MW01029560

THE

How **Stephen Curry**
Is Making All
the Right Moves—with
Humility and **Grace**

STEPH

MIKE YORKEY

SHILOH RUN PRESS
An Imprint of Barbour Publishing, Inc.

The author is represented by and this book is published in association with the literary agency of WordServe Literary Group, Ltd., www.wordserveliterary.com.

Published by Shiloh Run Press, an imprint of Barbour Publishing, Inc., P.O. Box 719, Uhrichsville, Ohio 44683, www.shilohrunpress.com

Our mission is to publish and distribute inspirational products offering exceptional value and biblical encouragement to the masses.

 Member of the
Evangelical Christian
Publishers Association

CONTENTS

The Golden State Warriors' Stephen Curry has elevated his game to stratospheric heights and reshaped the way basketball is played from his long-distance shooting to his penetrating slashes to the basket.

(AP PHOTO/BEN MARGOT)

INTRODUCTION

At the start of the 2010–11 NBA season, I (Mike Yorkey) received an assignment to write a book about Christian players in the league as part of the Playing with Purpose series.

After doing my research and working my sources, I realized that the pool wasn't very deep. In fact, I was hard-pressed to come up with a dozen National Basketball Association players who were serious about their faith and walking the talk. Since at any one time there are between 360 and 450 active players in the NBA (the 30 teams can carry as few as 12 and as many as 15 players), that meant a dozen committed Christians comprised a tiny fraction—around 3 percent—of those playing in the league.

My total didn't include a number of Christian players who, upon closer review, had succumbed to the many temptations that bounce into the laps of NBA athletes during a long season that runs from October until possibly June—and throughout the off-season as well. I believed they were men of faith, but they had a weakness for women and had fathered children out of wedlock. We all make mistakes, but I wanted to set the bar high, especially because my Playing with Purpose books reach a lot of impressionable young readers interested in learning more about their sports heroes.

In the midst of my research, however, I kept hearing good things about two players. They were teammates on the Golden State Warriors: Stephen Curry and Jeremy Lin.

In October 2010, Stephen was beginning his second year in the NBA after a successful rookie season in the Warriors backcourt. Jeremy, meanwhile, surprised the basketball world by taking the final roster spot as an undrafted free agent out of Harvard University, not exactly a hotbed of basketball talent.

Jeremy was getting tons of publicity—"trending" in the social media world—because he was the first Asian-American to step onto an NBA court. (A Japanese-

American player, Wataru Misaka, played just three games for the New York Knicks back in 1947 when the Knicks were part of the Basketball Association of America, or BAA.) Jeremy's crashing of the so-called "bamboo ceiling" in a sport dominated by black and white players was a feel-good story that Warriors' fans rallied around. I read how Oracle Arena, the Warriors' home court in Oakland, California, was populated with thousands of Asian-Americans eager to cheer on their trailblazing rookie. As the last man on the bench, however, Jeremy got most of his minutes during "garbage time"—the final few moments of lopsided wins or losses when starters like Stephen Curry came out and the game got sloppy and undisciplined.

At the time, during the 2010–11 season, Jeremy had a more interesting backstory than Stephen, so when I wrote *Playing with Purpose: Inside the Lives and Faith of Top NBA Stars*, I devoted a major chapter to Jeremy's pixie-dust journey from Palo Alto High in Silicon Valley to the highest echelon of professional basketball.

But I also appreciated Stephen Curry's long Christian testimony, one that began in fourth grade when he responded to an altar call at Central Church of God in Charlotte, North Carolina. That, and his sharpshooting skill from the perimeter as starting point guard for the Warriors, of course. I only devoted four pages to Stephen's story, but I included an anecdote of how, during his college days at Davidson, Stephen took a Sharpie pen and wrote "Romans 8:28" on his sneakers.

What a different life journey each player has taken in the last half-dozen years! I'll get to Stephen, but let me start with Jeremy. During the 2010–11 season, this Asian-American ballplayer was

- demoted to D League by the Warriors
- put on waivers before the start of the strike-shortened 2011–12 season
- picked up by the Houston Rockets
- released on Christmas Eve and out of the NBA

On the day after Christmas, Jeremy woke up at his parents' home, studied his Bible, and then drove to a nearby gym to stay in shape in case another NBA team wanted him. During his shootaround, he whispered to himself Romans 8:28—the same verse Stephen highlighted on his sneakers:

And we know that in all things God works for the good of those who love him, who have been called according to his purpose.

Little did Jeremy know what God had waiting for him. The New York Knicks picked him up, and in February 2012, Jeremy came off the bench to ignite a seven-game explosion that became known as "Linsanity." Overnight, Jeremy Lin became as famous as any NBA star, including LeBron James and Kobe Bryant. The Chinese media swooped in and turned Jeremy into a household name among the 1.3 billion inhabitants of the world's most populous country.

Meanwhile, back in the Bay Area, Jeremy's old teammate, Stephen Curry, was nearly forgotten, playing on lousy teams that averaged 28 wins a season his first three years in the NBA. Even more worrisome were the constant ankle injuries that threatened to cripple his career. Each time Stephen limped to the bench after turning an ankle—always his right—there were whispers that his body couldn't hold up to the demands of a brutal NBA schedule.

During the 2010–11 season, Stephen lost eight games to various ankle sprains. A month after the season was over, in May 2011, he underwent successful surgery in Charlotte, his hometown. Dr. Bob Anderson, a foot and ankle specialist who was the assistant team physician for the Carolina Panthers, repaired two balky ligaments in his right ankle.

Stephen pushed himself in rehab, but the 2011–12 season didn't start on time because of a player lockout. When an agreement was reached in December 2011, the players rushed into a condensed training camp. During a preseason game, Stephen turned his ankle again while defending Sacramento Kings guard Jimmer Fredette at the top of the key, where Fredette put on a crossover dribble move. Stephen hit the floor in pain, and the sight of him clinging to the shoulders of two teammates as he gingerly limped to the locker room was painful to witness.

Stephen missed a boatload of games, playing in only 26 regular-season contests in 2011–12—Jeremy's "Linsanity" year. Sportswriters wrote that Stephen's "taffy" ankles were held together by nuts, bolts, and prayers, which wasn't too far from the truth.

After missing 50 games in his first three NBA seasons, a consensus was forming around the league regarding Stephen's future: while he was praised as an amazing shooter and superb floor general, some coaches and scouts felt his right ankle was too suspect for the rigors of a full NBA schedule.

The Warriors, not winning many games and in a rebuilding mode, faced a major decision: Should they cut their losses and let Stephen go to restricted free agency or stay the course with Stephen as their cornerstone? Further complicating the Warriors' decision was Stephen's contract status, as NBA franchises can sign first-round picks to contract extensions after their third year in the league. (The Warriors had drafted Stephen in the first round of the 2009 draft, the seventh player chosen overall.) But the contract extension has to wrap up *before* the start of the fourth season.

Leading up to the 2012–13 season opener, Stephen was in the final year of his rookie contract. It would pay him $3.9 million, low by NBA standards. He was due for a major raise if the Warriors chose to extend his rookie contract—just how much would be decided at the negotiation table.

Both sides knew that Stephen could be paid as much as $15 million a year for four years—a total of $60 million—should the Warriors decide to lock him up. (These astronomical figures are decided by the NBA bargaining agreement and salary cap issues.) Both sides were aware that Stephen's ankle injuries mitigated that number, but how much of a discount was a matter of give-and-take as the contract extension deadline loomed. Stephen was dealing with ankle issues during preseason camp, which didn't strengthen his agent's hand in the negotiations, especially after head coach Mark Jackson decided to sideline Stephen until the start of the regular season.

Just before the first game, the two sides agreed to a four-year, $44 million contract. All the money was guaranteed, meaning that even if Stephen's sprained ankle never healed, he could lay on the beach with his young family for a *long* time. He would never have to punch a time clock.

At the end of the day, the rookie contract extension was about the risk each side was willing to accept. By coming to terms, the Warriors retained a deadeye shooter with tons of upside, at a reduced rate. Stephen, meanwhile, got three things he wanted: a chance to stay with the Warriors, financial security, and a

Steph can score—or pass—from anywhere on the court. His acrobatic moves place a lot of stress on a balky right ankle, which has occasionally kept him off the court.
(AP Photo/Marcio Jose Sanchez)

"reasonable" salary. Sure, $9.8 million a year was a nice bump from $3.9 million (and would rise to $12.1 million in the fourth and final year of the contract), but that didn't even place him among the Top 50 salaries among NBA players. It even left him as the fifth-highest paid member on his own team.

Bob Myers, in his first year as Golden State's general manager, said the Warriors showed confidence in Stephen and his suspect ankle by coming to terms with their star guard. "Clearly, because of his injury, there was more risk there," Myers said. "To not acknowledge that wouldn't be right. With him, the thinking from ownership on down was that if you're going to bet on a player, this was the type of player you bet on because of his character and because of his talent."

Stephen breathed a sigh of relief that he was staying in the Bay Area. "I can't thank the Warriors enough for opening up negotiations when they really didn't have to. I guess they saw the promise in my game and what I could do for a team."

With the contract extension behind him, it was apparent that Stephen had to find a better ankle brace, one that would reduce the risk of chronic injury but not compromise his full range of motion. Stephen tried several different models before finding exactly what he was looking for: the A2-DX ankle brace from Zamst, a high-performance sports equipment company. The A2-DX used a technology called Exo-Grid to provide a rigid exterior that would prevent his right ankle from rolling inward or outward.

Stephen liked how the A2-DX—which sells for around $53 on Amazon—allowed him to wear the same size Nike sneakers. (Today, Stephen plays in Under Armour basketball shoes, but more on that later.) "I make a lot of different cuts, and I feel secure in that when I put my foot in that brace, it's not going to go anywhere," he said. "It's a good feeling to have."

So, with no more ankle issues, the security of a four-year guaranteed contract, and an upgrade of talent on the Warriors team, Stephen was poised to take the NBA by storm. Throw in a solid marriage to his childhood sweetheart, Ayesha, and the birth of their first child (daughter Riley arrived on July 19, 2012), and you could call it Stephen Curry Unleashed.

In four short years, Stephen has reshaped the way basketball is played. He has been proclaimed the best shooter in basketball history and has the stats to back it up. He's been lauded by many experts as the best player on the planet and morphed into the (baby) face of the NBA. He led the Golden State Warriors to their first NBA championship in forty years during the 2014–15 season, has been named the NBA's most valuable player for each of the past two seasons, and has behaved in such a way that America has fallen head over heels in love with him and his endearing family.

Likable, humble, soft-spoken, and living out his faith—using words only when necessary—Stephen Curry is one of those nice guys you'd want to have a hamburger with or have your kids emulate. We feel like we're on a first-name basis with the young man, so much so that he's now known by the diminutive form of his first name: Steph.

"He's just a unique package," Pat Williams, the longtime senior vice president of the Orlando Magic, told me. "We really haven't seen anything like him. This kid is solid. He's got a great upbringing, strong parents, a strong Christian home. His faith is real, his marriage is strong, and he's got this little daughter who just entertains the world. It's amazing the crowds that come out to see him. When he came to Orlando, it was like Garth Brooks was in town or Michael Jordan had been reincarnated. It was just amazing to see the number of Curry jerseys and hear the buzz in the building, as well as the fervor to get close to him. I'm not sure we in the game were expecting it, but Steph has become a huge attraction and a real sports hero."

ANYONE HAVE A PRONUNCIATION GUIDE?

How do you pronounce Stephen Curry's first name?

The correct pronunciation is *Steff-in*, not *Steff-on* or *Steev-en*. But a Nike big shot botched it at a closed-door meeting with Steph after his shoe deal expired in 2013.

While pitching Stephen to stay with the iconic company, the Nike marketer talked about all the great things the brand could do for "Steph-on." No one from the Nike side corrected him.

Stephen and his father, Dell, were nonplussed—meaning they were stunned and dumbfounded. It felt like they were being disrespected.

Not long afterward, Steph chose to sign a shoe deal with Under Armour, which is described in greater detail in Chapter 6, "From Air Jordans to Curry Ones."

I bet everyone at Nike knows how to pronounce Stephen's name now.

WHY A BOOK LIKE
THE RIGHT STEPH?

Stephen Curry is the most-watched athlete on YouTube, and that's saying something when you think about the global audience for soccer stars like Lionel Messi or Cristiano Ronaldo or tennis players like Novak Djokovic and Roger Federer.

Every six months, Steph racks up another 150 million views on the video-streaming service, averaging around 1 million hours watched every month or 30,000 hours *every day*. That's an incomprehensible number of eyeballs, a testament to the way many people spend their free time these days.

Steph's most-watched video highlight, seen more than 8 million times, is a clip of him dribbling the ball on Kobe Bryant. The Lakers star plays him close and slaps at the ball, but Steph frees himself and launches the ball from a good four feet beyond the three-point line—"the other county" as the NBA Network announcer says on the video clip—then watches the ball swish through the net.

Steph has made such shots thousands of times, but what made that 2014 highlight go viral was Kobe's grin and playful slap of Steph's butt as the Warriors dropped back to defend their basket.

Beyond YouTube videos, there's also an insatiable demand for reading material on Steph, judging from the thousands of newspaper, magazine, and "fandom" articles and blogs that migrate onto the web. You can find at least sixteen books on Steph in the Amazon bookstore, but my glance at a number of sample chapters told me many of these tomes were short, noncompelling, Kindle-only unauthorized biographies.

The Right Steph is also an unauthorized biography, but this book is different—I'm writing about how Steph's strong faith is baked into his basketball career and the way he lives life and treats others. I have not interviewed Steph for this book because he will undoubtedly write his autobiography someday, and he's been instructed by his agent, Jeff Austin of Octagon, not to cooperate with book projects such as this one.

So until he works with a collaborator (*Hey, Steph, I'm available!*), I hope you'll enjoy this fascinating story in the meantime.

Pat came into the NBA in 1968—nearly fifty years ago—and has been general manager of four NBA teams. He's also written more than one hundred books on the topics of leadership, teamwork, and living a successful and rewarding life, so he's a student of people and the characteristics that make them great. Stephen, he believes, is in the prime of his career—and we would all do well to sit up and take notice.

"We're seeing him coming to a peak," Pat said. "We haven't seen anything quite like him in recent memory. His teams have been winning at an extraordinary clip the last two years. Are the Warriors going to win 70 games every year? It may happen because he's a team guy first. Stephen wants his team to do well, which is a beautiful thing. The San Francisco Bay Area is in a frenzy about the Warriors, but Stephen is also developing fans for the NBA who never paid attention to the game before. He's a lovable, good-looking kid who's respectful and polite to others. I don't think he has an ounce of jerk in him, and that's very attractive to fans."

So, America, sit back and enjoy the Steph Curry Experience—a once-in-a-lifetime sensory explosion. He's revolutionizing a popular game that brings together a basket, a leather ball, and a flick of the wrist from beyond the three-point line. What's even better is that he's playing for an audience beyond the millions of NBA fans—an audience of One. Steph Curry is playing to please God, who works for the good of those who love Him and have been called according to His purpose.

And that's pretty cool to see.

Steph is flanked by his proud parents, Dell and Sonya Curry, on June 26, 2009, when he was selected No. 7 overall in the NBA draft. Dell Curry was known as a deadeye shooter during a sixteen-season career in the NBA, mainly with the Charlotte Hornets. These days, Dell works as the color commentator on the Hornets television broadcasts, which makes games between the Hornets and the Warriors interesting to listen to.

1

HIS FATHER'S APPRENTICE

Whenever I write a sports biography, I like to focus on the family.

I don't say that because I was editor of *Focus on the Family* magazine for eleven years, although my time with the ministry founded by Dr. James Dobson greatly impacted my marriage and how my wife, Nicole, and I raised our children. I say it because the way parents bring up their children means everything to how their sons and daughters develop physically, mentally, and spiritually, and ultimately how they turn out as adults. The social upheavals and technological advances of the last twenty years have certainly made child rearing more difficult, but the ingredients of successful parenting—time, attention, and effort—never change.

Steph's parents, Dell and Sonya Curry, appear to have done everything right. Of course, we don't know what happened behind closed doors nor can we predict the future, but my confidence is high because we see the fruit of their parenting labors. As Matthew 7:16 (NLT) says: "You can identify them by their fruit, that is, by the way they act."

There's no doubt that Steph grew up in unusual circumstances. But they were unusual in a good way:

- Steph has off-the-chart athletic genes because he's the son of a professional basketball player and an athletic mother who played volleyball at Virginia Tech, a Division 1 school. Sonya's kin, the Snell family, is "perhaps the most athletically decorated bloodline" in Virginia's New River Valley, wrote Travis Williams in the *Roanoke Times*.

- Steph has an excellent spiritual foundation because Sonya, followed by Dell, committed their lives to Christ after Steph was born and reared him in the spirit of Proverbs 22:6 (NLT): "Direct your children onto the right path, and when they are older, they will not leave it."

- Finally, Steph was raised in a wealthy home, a fact that few commentators mention. His father was in his third season in the NBA when Steph was born, so Dell was making big bucks. By the time Steph was eight years old, Dell and Sonya had enough banked to afford a luxurious, six-bedroom, nine-bath, 8,305-square-foot residence situated on sixteen leafy acres in Providence Plantation, thirteen miles south of downtown Charlotte. The custom crib inside a gated community came with a shimmering pool that was perfect for cannonballs, a relaxing hot tub, and a snazzy outdoor basketball court appointed with glass backboards and surrounded by lights for night play. The court, painted green, even had a lane and three-point arc—from NBA range, of course. (I'm sure the game room was awesome and there were tons of toys in the bedrooms, too.)

In addition to the creature comforts, Steph was the beneficiary of experiences that most kids can only dream about: jetting off to NBA road games during school breaks, playing on youth travel teams in faraway states, receiving private schooling and extra coaching, and going on family vacations to exotic locales.

Growing up privileged can be a blessing or a curse. Sure, it's nice to have all that stuff and plenty of options and opportunities, but some youngsters surrounded by such a gilded environment become spoiled and lazy, feeling entitled to the finer things of life. We've all seen how some children of wealthy parents lack a desire to work hard, blissfully unaware of how good they have it. But Steph Curry has his head screwed on right, which is a credit to Dell and especially Sonya, the main parent on duty since her husband's demanding career in the NBA made him travel so much.

"She's a strong woman," Steph said of his mother. "She did a great job with me and my siblings. She deserves a lot of credit for how we turned out." Sonya kept a chore list on a kitchen board, made sure the homework got done, and stressed academics. The role of disciplinarian generally fell on Sonya's shoulders, who set the tone for how Steph and his younger brother, Seth, and younger sister, Sydel, were supposed to act.

One time Steph decided to test the boundaries, as kids are wont to do. He purposely didn't do the dishes, one of the chores written on the kitchen board. Sonya warned him that he couldn't practice or play the next game if that happened. This is how Steph described what happened next at his MVP acceptance speech in 2015:

> *If we didn't handle that business, there were no privileges. I remember sitting out my first middle school game because I didn't handle my stuff at home. That's a pretty embarrassing moment if you go to your first middle school game and you have to tell your team, "Hey, fellas, I can't play tonight. I didn't do the dishes." They're like,* What? What are you talking about? *So just that lesson taught me there is more to life than basketball.*

Lesson taken, lesson learned.

Sonya and Dell were intentional in the way they raised Steph, grounding him in family and faith. They taught him invaluable lessons in work ethic, respect for authority, treating others the way he would want to be treated, and looking people in the eye. These qualities come from a mother and father who modeled those traits themselves and weren't afraid to express their views.

For instance, one of his mother's pet peeves is athletes who wear sunglasses indoors. She's been around plenty of NBA players who won't take them off for anything, even while conducting postgame press conferences. To Sonya, sunglasses signaled to the outside world that the wearer is a rock star—and everyone else isn't.

"It says, *Look at me, I made it, I'm going to let you look at me,*" Sonya told the *Mercury News.* "But there's no connection. It's the aloofness."

Steph heeded his mother's admonition not to wear sunglasses indoors—until the time he strolled into the Warriors offices wearing a pair of dark shades. This happened shortly after he learned he had won his first NBA MVP award in May 2015.

Here's what happened next, according to Warriors general manager Bob Myers, who told the story at Steph's MVP award ceremony. "About a week ago," Myers began, "I saw him enter our facility with sunglasses on inside, and I think that's always the beginning of going in the wrong direction. So I told him that.

I said, 'Is this what we're doing now? We're doing this inside?' "

Chastened, the sunglasses came off. Good thing Mom wasn't around, or she would have grabbed Steph by the ear and set him straight first. Afterward, when Sonya heard what happened at the Warriors facility, she praised Myers for "calling out" Steph. . .and that was the last time he wore his sunglasses indoors.

Sonya has been known to send her son a "Hey, watch your tone" text if she sniffs any arrogance in Steph's postgame TV interviews. She reminds her son of the importance of humility and to be mindful of why he's in the unique position that he finds himself in, on top of the basketball world.

"We believe God opened the door for Stephen for a reason—to be a light and example of God," she said. That's why connecting with the fans is important, which starts with looking others in the eye, signing autographs, and not forgetting who put him there. Of course, Dell had also modeled that behavior during his playing days.

You may be wondering if there was any grand plan on Sonya and Dell's part to raise Steph to become a professional basketball player like his father. But that wasn't the case.

"We decided early on that we wouldn't focus on that with our kids," Sonya said. "I watched so many other children of players, young boys who just thought this life was automatically expected, and then didn't know what else to do. From the beginning, ours knew [basketball] was Daddy's job. I tried to keep it normal and grounded."

That wasn't easy to do since most of Steph's childhood revolved around the rhythms of his father's basketball career. Dell played in the NBA from the time Steph was born until he was an eighth grader.

What a great experience that had to have been! From October through May, Steph hung out in his father's locker room before and after home games, which had to be on weekends since Mom felt school nights were problematic. Young Steph shot baskets on the main floor before the arena opened to the public, was a fly on the wall as players dressed and kibitzed before games, and got another shootaround after the final buzzer, while he waited for his father to shower and answer questions from the media.

During the game, from his seat inside the cavernous arena, Steph was like a carpenter's son perched on a four-legged stool at his father's woodshop. At an impressionable age, he soaked in everything about the game—watching his father put moves on defenders, whip passes to his teammates, swish his shots, and get back on defense—never realizing that basketball fundamentals were becoming second nature to him.

This is how Michael Kruse of *Charlotte Magazine* described it:

> *When Dell was with the Hornets, and Stephen was a boy, Sonya would sit next to her son at games and ask him: "See your dad?"*
>
> *Stephen watched those games as a boy in a way that in retrospect was highly unusual. He didn't watch the ball. He watched his dad. What that meant was that he grew up watching the movements of a man who for a decade and a half was one of the world's very best shooters and users of screens. Stephen, of course, didn't think of it that way at the time. He was just a kid who wanted to watch his dad.*

Nobody knew it then, but Steph would be the apprentice who grew up to be just like his father—and his mother. The three remain close today. During the last two seasons, when the Warriors were in the midst of their playoff runs for the NBA championship, it was a given that Dell and Sonya would be in the house, watching their son play. They're a photogenic couple, still youthful in their early fifties, and they appear to enjoy themselves. (Though that's probably easy to do when your son is winning a lot and shooting the lights out of the building.)

So who are Dell and Sonya Curry? How did they meet? And why do they have an incredible story to tell about bringing Steph into this world?

FAMILY MATTERS

I'll start with Dell, who was born Wardell Stephen Curry on June 25, 1964. Dell grew up in Grottoes, Virginia, a quiet hamlet in the historic Shenandoah Valley that backs up to the base of the Blue Ridge Mountains. His father, also Wardell Curry, went by the name of Jack. His mother was named Juanita, but everyone called her Duckie.

THAT RICKETY RIM

When Steph would visit his grandparents growing up, he'd shoot for hours at the rickety rim, knowing that he, too, had to shoot swishes—or chase after the rebound. The unpredictable backboard and unforgiving rim necessitated an impossibly high, parabolic arc in order for the ball to sail cleanly through the basket. This was the genesis of the same high arc we see when Steph shoots from beyond the three-point line today.

His grandfather's unstable rim and shaky backboard became a visionary place for Steph. "Make it work no matter what you have to work with—that's something that stuck with me very early on," Steph told *ESPN The Magazine*. "Adjust. Get creative. Try a different angle, a different lane, a different move or a different shot—just make it work. Out there on my grandpa's court, there was no better place in the world to breed that kind of creativity."

This side-of-the-road backboard is where Steph got his love for the really long ball. He'd stand on the kitchen step, where the rim wasn't visible, launching two-handed 50-foot shots over the corner of the house.

And now you know where his legendary pregame "tunnel shots" at Oracle Arena come from.

Jack supported the family as a day-shift machinist at a General Electric factory in nearby Waynesboro, so they were a blue-collar family. (Duckie also worked shifts at the plant.) As a young boy, Dell was given chores that included tending to the family's large garden and keeping the rows meticulously straight and free of weeds.

Dell's father put up a basketball rim along a dirt road, securing a fiberglass standard to a splintery wooden utility pole with steel brackets that had plenty of give. Because the backboard and rim were so wobbly, the goal was unforgiving. Dell had to swish the ball through the net or watch his shot clang off the rim and skitter down the road. It was "make it or chase it" growing up, which has a way of concentrating your mind for the task at hand.

The story goes that during the summer, while his parents were punching a time clock at the GE plant, Dell's four older sisters—he was the youngest of five children—would herd him out of the house, toss him a basketball, and tell him not to come back until lunchtime. Then they'd lock the door and binge-watch TV sitcoms and soap operas.

Dell didn't have much else to do but shoot baskets and play "pretend" games against himself as he took shot after shot at the loose backboard. A respite came when his father arrived home from work to rebound Dell's shots and rifle him chest passes for the next jumper. And he would frequently offer a critique of Dell's shooting form.

When Dell got older, he started riding his bike to the rural property of the local high school basketball coach, Don Landes, who had a much firmer basketball rim inside his barn. The coach took an interest in Dell—and who wouldn't after seeing how much this youngster wanted to practice? Dell was given a key and the freedom to go to the barn anytime to work on his shooting. When Coach Landes was there, he worked with Dell to square up his shoulders, form an L with his shooting elbow, and snap his wrist on the follow-through with the ball coming off the fingertips. Dell told himself that he couldn't leave until he made 500 shots.

That barn became Dell's laboratory, a place where he could practice in the fall and winter when rain, sleet, and snow drove everyone indoors. Shot after shot, swish after swish, Dell developed his shooting stroke, holding his follow-through until the ball hit the floor. The quick release, the moves off the dribble, and the penetration of the lane were fundamentals that were honed by countless hours of practice.

As Dell started playing organized basketball, showing off his deadeye shooting skill, folks told the youngster that he had a gift—and he had to nurture it. Dell began thinking that maybe basketball would be his ticket out of the Virginia countryside. Or maybe baseball pitching since he was also quite a moundsman growing up. He hoped either game would provide a college scholarship and a brighter future than being a machinist like his dad.

Basketball was Dell's sport, though. There was no three-point line when he played at Fort Defiance High School in the early 1980s, but he could fill a bucket from anywhere. Dell grew into the perfect size for a guard, at 6 feet, 4 inches. Being named as a McDonald's All-American in 1982 led to Virginia Tech offering him a full-ride hoops scholarship, but Dell's ability to hurl a baseball prompted scouts to show up at games during the spring of his senior year. Even though the Texas Rangers knew basketball was his first love, they tossed a 14th round draft selection at him, just to see if he would bite. Dell said no but became one of those rare two-sport athletes during his four years at Virginia Tech, playing basketball in the fall and winter and turning out for the baseball team when the hoops season was over.

Playing at the Division 1 level was an eye-opener. If Dell was going to succeed at Virginia Tech, he needed an even quicker release. "I could always shoot because I worked on it, but. . .I wasn't the fastest guy, couldn't jump the highest, so I knew I had to get my release off quicker," Dell said.

Dell worked on getting his knees bent and feet aligned with the basket a split second before he caught the ball, eliminating wasted movement in his shot delivery, and releasing the ball just before the top of his jump, all the while keeping his eyes locked on the rim.

His dazzling jump shot is why the Utah Jazz took Dell in the first round of the 1986 NBA Draft, the 15th player selected. (Baseball's Baltimore Orioles had selected Dell in the 14th round of the 1985 draft, but basketball was always going to be his game.)

As Dell left Blacksburg for Salt Lake City and the NBA, his heart pined for a Virginia Tech volleyball player named Sonya Adams. They would remain in contact.

A MELTING POT

Sonya Adams Curry is more of a mystery than Dell. Various newspaper clips and Internet musings say that she's part African-American, part Haitian, and part Caucasian. Others have said she's African-American Creole, which can be a mix of African-American, Spanish-American, French American, and Native American peoples—a real melting pot.

There's no doubt that she's fairly light skinned, which is where Steph gets his complexion. Sonya grew up in Radford, Virginia, a college town of 15,000 in the New River Valley and home to Radford University. I mentioned earlier that she is part of the famed Snell family, noted for its athletic prowess. Her cousins, Sidney Snell and Donald Wayne Snell, were top receivers on the Virginia Tech Hokies football team in the late 1970s and early 1980s, respectively.

Sonya's mother, Candy, comes from the Snell line. She married Cleive E. Adams and had four children that included Sonya, who was born May 30, 1966. Cleive and Candy divorced when Sonya was young, so she basically grew up in a single-parent home.

Sonya first laid eyes on Dell—or at least his picture—when she was in high school. Her mother happened to bring home a program from the Virginia Tech basketball team, and one of the players caught her eye. "He's the kind of man I'd like to marry," she said, pointing to the head shot of Dell Curry.

Sonya was a standout volleyball and basketball player at Radford High, so it was a natural for her to follow in her cousins' footsteps and play for the home state Hokies. Sonya was only 5 feet, 3 inches, a disadvantage on the basketball court but a good height for being a setter on a volleyball team. She enrolled at Virginia Tech in August 1984 and went right into practice for volleyball, a fall sport.

The volleyball team shared a practice gym with the basketball squad. Perhaps Sonya and Dell bumped into each other at the water fountain during a break from practice. Maybe it was a glance from across the gym, but somehow, the two connected. It's not difficult to imagine that Dell was smitten with a gorgeous young woman. And Sonya was certainly attracted to Dell, two years older and wearing a cute mustache. When they went out on a date and found out that they had each grown up in the New River Valley, the comfort level likely shot up several notches. They continued dating, becoming an item on campus.

In my research of Sonya, I found out she was a very good volleyball player. In the 1999 Virginia Tech media guide, there's a photo of Sonya next to the "Single Season/Career Records" section, which noted that in 1986, her junior season, she tallied 57 aces, sixth-most in Virginia Tech history. She was also the first player listed among the "All-Time Letter Winners," which noted that she won a letter for the 1984, '85, and '86 seasons.

What happened to 1987? Why didn't she play her senior year?

Sonya Adams was pregnant.

Stephen was born on March 14, 1988, so if you measure back nine months, he was conceived in the latter half of June 1987, following Dell's rookie season with the Utah Jazz.

As for why Wardell Stephen Curry II was born in Akron, Ohio—reportedly at the same hospital as LeBron James—it's because Dell had been traded from Utah to the Cleveland Cavaliers just before the start of the 1987–88 season. Dell and Sonya made their home in Akron, forty miles south of Cleveland.

Which led to my next question: When did Dell and Sonya marry?

Various news sites on the Internet say that Dell and Sonya were married in 1988. None listed an exact date, and my efforts to search marriage license records came up with zilch as well. Whatever the date, Sonya would already have been five or six months into her pregnancy when New Year's Day arrived.

I called Joshua Cooley, who'd recently written a cover story on Steph for the Fellowship of Christian Athletes' *FCA Magazine*. Maybe he could shed some light on my question.

After telling Josh what I learned, he told me that he had interviewed Dell and Sonya twice. Once in February 2011—"before Steph blew up," Josh said—and again in March 2016, in conjunction with a cover story on Steph that appeared in the May/June 2016 issue of *FCA Magazine*.

"In February 2011," Josh said, "I asked Dell if he and Sonya met at Virginia Tech, and my transcription says, 'I met her in 1985. We dated for several years. We married in 1988, and it will be twenty-three years this August.' I took this to mean August 2011 since this interview was in February and the math worked out."

In other words, Dell and Sonya married when Steph was five months old.

I think Dell and Sonya should get a ticker-tape parade down Broadway, be feted with every award you can imagine, and be told thank you for what they did—for carrying Steph to term and giving him life.

Let's be real: this was a crisis pregnancy that could have ended far differently and no one would have been the wiser. Yes, Sonya did have to forgo her senior year of volleyball, but she and Dell did the right thing—they kept the baby and got married. That wasn't the easy route, but as they say, love won out.

Think of what this world would be *without* Steph in our lives. It really is mind-boggling to consider since he has brought so much joy to millions of people through his basketball skills.

"I think it's a wonderful testimony, what Dell and Sonya did, regardless of who the baby was or what he or she turned out to be," Josh said. "I will always be in favor of life. I was adopted, so I know what that means. But when you add that it turned out to be Steph Curry, who is currently the best basketball player in the world, hopefully that drives the message home for some people because of Steph's notoriety and fame."

Here's another reason why I think so highly of how Dell and Sonya handled this crisis pregnancy: neither were tracking with the Lord at the time!

Yes, we all know that Steph was raised in a Christian home and accepted Christ when he was fourteen years old. We know that he attended Charlotte

Christian in his high school years. But his parents didn't decide to follow Christ until Steph was in early elementary school.

In Josh's February 2011 interview with Sonya, she said this:

> For me, I grew up in the church. My grandmother always used to make us go. Around twelve or so, I went through the confirmation class at church and got baptized there. I then went off to college, where I lost track of my walk. My relationship with the Lord waned in college.

So when did she become a committed follower of Christ?

Sonya said that in 1994, when Steph was six years old, the family was attending some church services, but there wasn't a whole lot of spiritual fruit in their lives. "That's when she said she rededicated her life to the Lord," Josh told me. "This happened at a time when she said they were having some challenges in their marriage."

"What about Dell?" I asked Josh.

"Dell said he was playing in Toronto in 2000 when a former teammate of his, Bobby Phills, lost control of his Porsche and was killed in a car wreck," Josh continued. "When Dell went to the funeral, it really struck him that life was too short and he decided to change his life," Josh said.

Shortly after, Dell and Sonya started pulling from the same spiritual rope. Two years later, their oldest child, Steph, decided that he wanted what they had—and it wasn't basketball stardom or athletic glory.

It was a relationship with a Savior.

Steph was a baby-faced, twenty-one-year-old rookie when he stripped the ball from Dallas Mavericks forward Dirk Nowitzki early in the 2009-10 season. (AP Photo/Sharon Ellman)

2

SHOOTING FROM THE HIP

When Steph was a few months old, the NBA welcomed two new teams to the league—the Charlotte Hornets and the Miami Heat—which were allowed to pick and choose players from other teams. In the 1988 Expansion Draft, the Hornets made Dell Curry their second choice, plucking him away from the Cleveland Cavaliers.

In Charlotte, Dell filled a valuable role as the sixth man, coming off the bench to provide some offensive firepower. He had a silky-smooth perimeter game and became known for launching long jump shots—and making them with extraordinary consistency. Dell initiated the flight of the ball with hands so huge that he could palm it like Dr. J or Michael Jordan.

When you're a pure shooter who can score in bunches, coaches will always find a spot on the team for you. Dell turned out to be a perfect fit for the Hornets, who were the city's first professional sports franchise. Locals went loco for their Hornets: the Charlotte Coliseum, which seated 24,042 fans, hosted 364 consecutive NBA sellouts from December 1988 to November 1997.

During a ten-year career with the Hornets, Dell played in nearly every one of those games, which doesn't happen often in the NBA unless you're known around the league by your first name. Staying in one city allowed Dell and Sonya to put down roots, become part of the community, and complete their family: Seth was born in 1990, and Sydel came along in 1994.

Steph was first in the birth order, which greatly affects personality. Dr. Kevin Leman, a Christian psychologist and author of *The Birth Order Book*, said firstborns are natural leaders who tend to be reliable, conscientious, and perfectionistic. They don't like surprises.

From a young age, Steph was goal oriented. As soon as he could stand on his own two feet, he was wobbling toward a plastic Fisher-Price basketball hoop his parents set up in the living room. At that age, kids don't shoot—but they quickly learn what the goal is: jam the ball through the hoop. Grandma Duckie offered a running commentary from the couch, doing the play-by-play as Steph waddled his way to the rack to dunk the ball. He was one of those relentless kids with a ball in his hands.

Eventually, Steph grew big enough to shoot a real leather ball at a real steel rim painted in orange. But when he started elementary school, he was among the shortest kids in his class, so it took all of his might to launch the ball.

At the private elementary school he attended, Steph knew the headmaster very well—because she was his mother! Sonya, with an assist from Dell, founded the Christian Montessori School of Lake Norman in 1995, when Steph was seven years old. An aunt, India Adams, was his teacher, and his grandmother Candy Adams was the school cook. The school's opening happened a year after Sonya, who'd earned a degree in elementary education and a minor in family studies, had made a commitment to Christ, so she was moving quickly to put her faith into action.

The Montessori approach is for children to learn on their own while being guided by a teacher. That method appealed to Sonya, who believed in curriculum that was geared toward developing creative, independent children with an enthusiasm for learning. Because this was a Christian version of a Montessori school, godly values and lessons were also taught.

Basketball and baseball were the big sports for Steph in his elementary school years. Regarding the latter, Steph wasn't a pitcher like his dad but a good fielder and line-drive hitter. But growing up with a father playing in the NBA was always going to tilt the scales toward the court. Hanging around humongous professional basketball players—your dad's friends—had to be a kick for a little kid.

At the Charlotte Coliseum, the player that Steph looked up to the most was the shortest ever to play in the NBA—5-foot, 3-inch Muggsy Bogues, a whirling dervish on the court. There's a famous YouTube video of Muggsy giving four-year-old Steph an "airplane ride" through the locker room.

The Curry boys were fixtures in the players' dressing area. "Every coach they had welcomed the family atmosphere and having me and Seth coming around. I remember waiting in the tunnel, hanging out until they were done shooting so we could go out and throw up some shots," Steph said.

"Throw up" is a good description because Steph first had to bring the ball down to his right hip to generate enough force to launch the ball above the rim. Basically, he was shooting from his waist in elementary school—but he was deadly accurate and way better than his peers.

Page Moir, Dell's teammate at Virginia Tech, partnered with Dell to run summer basketball camps in Charlotte and at Roanoke College in Virginia. "When Stephen was five, he could play with the eight-year-olds," Moir said. "Even at that age, he was a superstar with all the kids in the camp."

At a Nike Hoop Summit high school all-star game in 1996, eight-year-old Steph played in a halftime exhibition and stole the show. A *Charlotte Observer* reporter wrote this at the time:

> With Dell on the sidelines applauding, Stephen dazzled, wearing an oversized Reggie Miller No. 31 Indiana Pacers jersey. He started fast breaks, created turnovers, dribbled through his legs, whipped behind-the-back passes, and nailed jumpers, including a long-distanced splash with seconds left that brought a roaring response from the crowd.

Reggie Miller, a shooting guard, and Steve Nash, a point guard with the Phoenix Suns, were Steph's idols at the time. A year later, Steph started playing on AAU (Amateur Athletic Union) travel teams. He also worked with a private coach—not because Dell wasn't available but because, at that age, it's sometimes better for Dad to be Dad. "He never really coached me like that, to be honest," Steph said. "He wasn't one of those drill-sergeant dads that bangs on your door and says it's time to go to work. It was more that he told us how important it was to have a work ethic."

Every spring during these years, Steph was still playing baseball, and that would have a huge impact on his basketball career for reasons nobody could have foreseen. When he was ten, Stephen was a starter on a youth baseball team that won the North Carolina state championship. One of his teammates was a Brendan McKillop. Keep track of that last name.

Also at age ten, Steph did something that would have eternal ramifications—and greatly impact the man he is today. In a first-person column published in

FCA Magazine, Steph said,

> I remember it like it was yesterday, the day I gave my life
> to Christ. I was in fourth grade, and I recall hearing and
> understanding the gospel of Jesus Christ and walking
> down the aisle to give my life to Him. My parents continued
> to pour into my faith from that point on, making sure I
> understood the commitment I'd just made. Starting in
> middle school, I attended Charlotte Christian School, which
> allowed me to hear the gospel on a daily basis. Looking
> back, my childhood was filled with the Lord's presence.

In the summer of this same year, the NBA team owners and players' union couldn't agree on a collective bargaining agreement. The players would be locked out from July 1, 1998, to January 20, 1999.

During this time, the Charlotte Hornets chose not to re-sign Dell, who was a free agent. He left the city as one of the team's most popular players, respected for his civic involvement—Dell had appeared at charity fundraisers, spoken at sports banquets, and held basketball camps. He departed as the Hornets' all-time leader in games played, total points scored, three-point field goals made and attempted, and three-point percentage. Dell had been the face of the franchise, and Curry jerseys—No. 30 in teal—populated SouthPark Mall.

When the lockout ended, Dell signed with the Milwaukee Bucks for a shortened, 50-game season and then found greener pastures in Toronto in the fall of 1999. Steph was eleven years old and starting middle school when Dell joined the Raptors. The elder Curry would play his final three seasons with Toronto, and the family moved to Canada for Dell's final season in 2001-02. Steph's parents enrolled him at Queensway Christian College for eighth grade.

Steph, thirteen at the time, was still small for his age, built like a celery stick, and sporting an angelic face. Local rules prevented him from playing varsity, so Steph suited up for the middle school team, draped with a mustard-yellow jersey that looked four sizes too big and shorts that hung down to his ankles.

Because Steph was four levels better than the competition, his team won every game—but against one rival, Queensway was down by six points with

As one of the NBA smaller players at 6 feet, 3 inches, Steph relies on quickness and speed to thread his way through and past tenacious defenders.

(AP Photo/Gerald Herbert)

just one minute to go. Coach James Lackey called a time-out. For most of the game, the bigger players on the visiting team had pushed Steph all over the court, triple-teaming him at times to slow him down.

Lackey was out of ideas. "Look, I don't know what to tell you," he said to the sweaty middle schoolers huddled around him. "Do you have a suggestion here? Help me out."

The coach was greeted by silence.

Then there was a Hollywood-style *Hoosiers* moment when Steph raised his hand. "Give me the ball," he said in a voice that had yet to deepen. "Give me the ball and we'll win."

"You heard him," the coach barked. "Give him the ball and get out of the way."

And it was another Hollywood finish: Steph rained a trio of threes on step-back jumpers from beyond the arc, scoring nine points to secure the victory. In helping the Saints finish the season undefeated, Steph *averaged* 50 points a game—Wilt (the Stilt) Chamberlain numbers. Coach Lackey said Steph was more than a gunner. "I couldn't believe his knowledge of the game at such a young age," Lackey said. "He knew movements of players and where they were going to be—he could see those passing lanes in a way that a guy his size normally can't."

When he wasn't burning the nets or running the fast break at Queensway, Steph was being his precocious self during afternoon shootarounds at the empty 19,800-seat Air Canada Centre. When the players were finished with their shooting drills, Steph would challenge 6-foot, 6-inch guard Vince Carter to one-on-one contests. Vince was an NBA All-Star and winner of the Slam Dunk Contest, so this was a lark-in-the-park diversion for him—but he made the pick-up games fun and instructive.

"He taught me great lessons," Steph said of Vince. "I remember how he treated me, and how much fun he had playing one-on-one for five, ten minutes after they practiced. It showed the humanity of an NBA player and the influence they can have. That rubbed off on me in a great way."

Believe it or not, Vince turns forty during the 2016–17 season and is *still* playing. I can only imagine the knowing looks he and Steph exchange every time they step onto an NBA hardwood together.

BACK ON HOME COURT

When the 2001–02 season was over, Dell retired. At age thirty-seven, after sixteen seasons in the NBA, he had left everything on the court—and he deserved to kick up his aching feet and rest those golden shooting arms. The family moved back to Charlotte and re-enrolled Steph, now a ninth grader, at Charlotte Christian School. Dell, suddenly with a lot of time on his hands, volunteered to be the assistant coach of the freshman team.

"He was just this little, small-type kid," said Shonn Brown, the varsity coach. Shonn could tell that Steph was way advanced for his age, but when he shot, he was still winging it from the hip—there was no other way for him to get the ball to the rim. "He could hoist it up there pretty good. . .he had really good accuracy," Shonn recalled. "Well, what would you expect? His father was a shooter."

Steph was 5 feet, 6 inches tall in the ninth grade, which isn't unusual. But his baby face made him look several years younger. Woe to any opponent who underestimated him.

The kid practiced nonstop. Dell had been careful not to be a pushy dad, but when Steph hit high school, it was like somebody flipped a switch in him—Steph wanted to be a baller, to use a slang term popular at the time. He couldn't wait to go to the gym after school and work on his shooting and ballhandling skills. If the weather was good after dinner, he'd play with Seth on their backyard court, lit for night play.

This was a time when Steph was stepping up in the area of faith as well. There were "devotional" times before school, when one of his parents would share a verse or two around the breakfast table, talking about what they could learn from God's Word. Dell and Sonya made sure they were in church every Sunday morning and drove Steph and his siblings back again on Wednesdays for youth group. The family attended Central Church of God, a Pentecostal megachurch with 6,000 members in southeastern Charlotte.

On the physical side, Steph was growing—inch by inch. He measured 5 feet, 8 inches in his sophomore year but weighed only 125 pounds.

Beanpole. Rail thin. His Knights uniform—he wore No. 30 in honor of his father—hung on him like his bony shoulders were a wire hanger. He didn't put on much weight when he hit his growth spurt going into his junior year—reaching 5 feet, 11 inches.

In the midst of this notable feature of adolescence, Dell decided that Steph's jump shot needed to be overhauled. His flip from the hip wouldn't cut the mustard against taller, faster defenders.

Dell was still a volunteer assistant coach at Charlotte Christian. One day at the gym, he pulled his son aside. Steph was clearly hungry to play basketball in college, but to reach the next level, he would have to move the release point of his shot above his head.

This may sound easy to do—*Hey, son, just release the ball higher*—but changing a shooting stroke is like adjusting a golf swing or a tennis forehand: it's hard to change muscle memory. For Steph, it was like starting over. His father tutored him on lifting the ball to the right place, raising his elbows so as to elevate his release point, guiding the ball with the predominant hand (the right in Steph's case), flicking his wrist when the ball was in the air, and holding his right arm high with wrist extended in a swanlike follow-through until the ball swished through the net.

The father-son workouts in the gym and in the backyard were relentless. There were 6 a.m. sessions, plus watching film of his new technique. This is where the hard work happened, the effort that would turn Steph from a very good shooter at the high school level to a world-class shot artist in a very short time. With Dell standing under the basket chest-passing the ball for Steph's next jumper, father and son worked tirelessly together nearly every day during the summer before his junior year.

Steph was playing on travel teams, and at first, the shots were finding the bottom of the net like they used to. He was making progress, and he left a good impression at the Nike Hoop Jamboree in St. Louis for the nation's Top 100 junior players.

The junior year is when college basketball coaches begin zeroing in on their elite recruits. Fortunately, Steph's overhauled shooting technique blossomed with the start of the high school season. In the final of the Chick-fil-A Classic tournament, Steph and Charlotte Christian were matched up against Norcross High, a team loaded with seven Division 1 recruits, including Jodie Meeks, who's played for the Milwaukee Bucks, Philadelphia 76ers, Los Angeles Lakers, and Detroit Pistons.

Steph controlled the floor, made the tough shots, slashed inside for layups, and single-handedly led the Knights to an unexpected victory. College recruiters sitting in the stands, however, yawned. They didn't think Steph had the height or the body size to withstand the rigors of D-1 basketball. They also noted that Steph had big feet—he was pushing size 14—that made him look less nimble than he really was.

There was really one school Steph wanted to attend: Virginia Tech. That was his parents' alma mater, the place where his pop made a name for himself and extended family members had played their ball. But the Hokie coaching staff wasn't excited about Steph. Rivals.com, a website that focuses on college football and basketball recruiting, gave him a modest three-star rating. Basketball coaches along the Atlantic Seaboard took their cues.

"Sometimes, kids don't pass the eye test," said Shonn Brown, who said that going into his senior year, Steph looked like he was about fourteen years old.

Too bad the recruiters couldn't see into his heart.

MAKING A PLAY

One person who trusted what he saw was Bob McKillop, head basketball coach at Davidson College, a private liberal arts school with only 1,700 students. The school was around thirty miles from the Curry home in southwest Charlotte, which was a bonus. Davidson basketball was traditionally a force in the Southern Conference, but it was one of the smallest schools with a Division 1 program. Call it the Butler of the South.

McKillop knew exactly who Steph was. After all, his son, Brendan, had once played on a championship baseball team with a ten-year-old Steph. During Steph's freshman year at Charlotte Christian, McKillop began sniffing around. His interest rose throughout Steph's sophomore year and was on fire by the time Steph was a junior.

We're going to build our program around you. . .you're a starter from Day 1. . . your parents can see every home game. . .you can even go home on weekends.

Even though the big Atlantic Coast Conference schools—Duke, North Carolina, Maryland—were taking a pass, McKillop found competition from similar small schools like Elon, Wofford, William & Mary, Winthrop, Virginia

Commonwealth, and High Point.

Steph had added some meat to his spindly bones—ten to fifteen pounds. During the summer before his senior year, he played in some high-level pickup games in downtown Charlotte against NBA talent (it helps to have connections) and more than held his own. At an AAU camp in Las Vegas, Steph wasn't considered a top player and therefore wasn't invited to compete on the main court. Nonetheless, McKillop was in the stands of an auxiliary court that day, hoping to make sure no major college coaches tried to poach a recruit he'd been trying to land for three years.

Steph had a bad game, dribbling the ball off his foot, passing out of bounds, and looking generally awful. He committed a slew of turnovers—something like ten.

"And I'm watching him," McKillop said, "and I see it. Through it all, he never once stopped playing defense. He never stopped listening to the coach. He never once pointed at a teammate. He never once even looked up at the referee to say he made a bad call. He just continued to play with the same intensity and enthusiasm. That's when I first thought, *Wait a minute here. We might have something even better than we had hoped.*"

In the fall of 2005, McKillop put a full-court press on Steph. He knew how good Steph was and how good he could be. He *really* wanted him.

Before making a verbal commitment, the Curry family wanted to be sure that playing at Virginia Tech was off the table. An intermediary, Page Moir, phoned Tech head coach Seth Greenberg and did the soft sell. . .*this kid is really coming along. . .you're going to regret passing on him. . . .*

Moir was told that all the scholarship money had been committed, but if Steph wanted to come to Virginia Tech as a walk-on, he'd get a good look. He could redshirt his first season and save a year of eligibility.

Steph didn't do redshirt. No way was he sitting *anywhere*.

The walk-on idea rankled the whole Curry clan. Even though Dell and Sonya could easily afford the out-of-state tuition, they knew that walk-ons are treated like. . .walk-ons. Nonscholarship players have too many strikes against them, including the perception that they weren't good enough to earn a full ride.

Ah, thanks but no thanks.

In November 2005, Coach McKillop showed up at the Curry house with his assistant Matt Matheny. As they say in business, they made their best-and-final pitch and then asked for the sale.

"And all of a sudden," McKillop told Joe Posnanski of NBC Sports, "Steph stands up and announces that he wants to come to Davidson. I was speechless for a second. Dell and Sonya were speechless for a second; I don't think they had any idea he was going to say that. And then we embraced as if we had been teammates forever.

"And I remember this clearly. As we were departing, Sonya says to me, 'Don't worry, we're going to fatten him up.' And I told her, 'Sonya, we'll take him just the way he is.' "

And Steph would put Davidson basketball on the map.

Steph is always playing with his mouthpiece during lulls in the action, especially when he is shooting free throws.
(AP Photo/ Marcio Jose Sanchez)

3

HELLO, BASKETBALL WORLD

There was no thought of redshirting Steph when he arrived on the Davidson campus, especially after fall practice started.

"Wait until you see Stephen Curry," Bob McKillop told a booster luncheon gathering, describing how he was "blown away" by Steph's skill level and basketball acumen during preseason practice. The hand-eye coordination necessary to bury shot after shot and the foot-eye coordination that gave Steph a whoosh-like step on his opponents were way above any expectations the silver-haired coach had harbored. With a mix of incredible shooting, competitive fire, and quiet confidence—all tempered by humility—Steph was a three-star "steal." McKillop told anyone who would listen—alumni, the media, and Davidson fans—just you wait. . .Steph is something special.

Often, the burden of expectations can weigh heavily on eighteen-year-old shoulders, but McKillop sang Steph's praises because (1) he believed the young man was an incredible basketball player for his age and (2) he thought Steph could handle it.

Steph moved into an on-campus apartment with Bryant Barr, Steve Rossiter, and Dan Nelms—teammates who would be his roommates for the next three years. He showed up with a microwave oven, his laptop, four duffel bags filled with clothes and basketball gear, and a red-white-and-blue quilt his grandmother had given him as a graduation gift.

Declaring himself a sociology major, Steph quietly blended into the college scene. He showed up at women's soccer games and occasionally dropped in at a frat party to be social—but he was no partier. In his spare time, he preferred to play the Wii Rock Band video game with his roomies, banging the "drums."

Right at six feet and slim as a Gumby character, Steph looked a bit overmatched in his first college game, committing eight turnovers in the opening half at Eastern Michigan. That was a major reason why Davidson trailed by 16 points at the break. McKillop thought about sitting Steph after intermission but decided to leave him in. During the second half, Steph coughed up the ball another five times, but guess what? He led the Wildcats to a come-from-behind victory while scoring 15 points. The following night, against Michigan—yes, the Maize and Blue in Ann Arbor—Steph dialed it up with 32 points, even though small-fry Davidson lost by 10.

Steph looked so young that he took a razzing from fans during road games. At a Christmas tournament his freshman year, a leather-lunged fan at the University of Tennessee at Chattanooga yelled out, "Hey, number 30! This is a college game! You're not old enough to be out there!"

A few long-distance three-pointers, dribble-drives through the lane for finger-roll layups, and sleight-of-hand steals silenced vocal fans like him. Meanwhile, basketball pundits started to take notice of Steph and his Davidson team because they won a *lot* of games to capture the Southern Conference championship and qualify for the NCAA tournament. Alas, Steph and the Wildcats lost to fourth-seeded Maryland in the first round of March Madness. Davidson finished the season 29–5.

Overall, it was a great season for young Steph. But I think the best thing that happened to him that year occurred just before his first practice in the fall.

Sonya had sent her son a text, saying she wanted to share her favorite Bible verse with him—a part of scripture that would offer motivation and encouragement. The verse was Romans 8:28, which I mentioned in the Introduction. It says God works out all things for the good of those who love Him.

And then Sonya said something else in her text. She urged her son to find a new verse that he could take hold of, one he could make his own "life verse."

Steph had taken Bible classes at Charlotte Christian and heard plenty of youth speakers preach during his teen years, so he was familiar with scripture. He chose Philippians 4:13: "I can do all things through Christ who strengthens me," as it's worded in the New King James Version.

"Philippians 4:13 was one that I thought about when I started to play basketball all the time," he said.

Shortly after choosing his life verse, Steph happened to be in the Davidson locker room, where the team manager presented him with his first pair of team shoes—a pair of Nikes. Steph had an idea: he found a black Sharpie and picked up one of his squeaky new shoes, holding it in his lap. Then he wrote "Romans 8:28" on one side of the shoe—aiming for the white rubber strip between the sole and the leather upper. Then he grabbed the other shoe and printed "I Can Do All Things," the first half of Philippians 4:13. "I thought that would be a good daily reminder to have it on my shoes," he said.

Mom made another suggestion worth noting. Sonya recommended that her son devise some outward sign that would become an internal reminder that God gets the glory for his success on the basketball court.

Steph thought about it and came up with a motion that felt both natural and freeing. Early in his freshman year, running onto the floor when the starting lineups were announced, he found his mother in the stands and tapped his chest twice with his right hand. Then he pointed his right index finger skyward. Sonya smiled and repeated the gesture back to him.

It wasn't long before Steph started tapping his chest and pointing upward after making his long, high-arcing rainbow jump shots or kissing the glass on "runner" drives to the basket. Today, the light-thump-to-the-chest and index-finger-to-the-sky is his trademark move. "I love to point people toward the Man who died for our sins on the cross," he said in a column he wrote for the Fellowship of Christian Athletes. "I know I have a place in heaven waiting for me because of Him, and that's something no earthly prize or trophy could ever top."

Yes, to God be the glory. "Basically it means 'have a heart for God,'" Steph said. "It keeps the perspective for me, why I play the game and where my strength comes from. It's been a good kind of grounding."

Let me point out one other interesting thing that Steph did during his freshman year. After home games, which almost always ended in victory since Davidson won 13 of 14 playing at the 5,223-seat Belk Arena, Steph and his teammates traipsed to the Student Union to hang out with their friends and meet other students. Anyone could come up and talk to him. "You can sit down and have a conversation with [the other students] and thank them for coming to the game," Steph said. "I don't think you really get that at a big school where the athletes kind of go missing from game to game."

Steph actually showing up at the Student Union and thanking his peers for coming out to cheer for him and the team?

That boggles the mind just as much as his acrobatic moves on the court.

BRACKET BUSTER

If Steph's freshman year was an introduction to the national stage, his sophomore year is when he crashed the party. He certainly messed up a lot of March Madness brackets.

After posting a perfect 20-0 record in the Southern Conference—and losing only a handful of games to name programs like North Carolina, Duke, UCLA, and North Carolina State—the Steph-led Davidson Wildcats qualified for March Madness again.

A first-round win over Gonzaga was an unexpected surprise. It was Davidson's first NCAA postseason win in nearly forty years, since 1969. Steph did his usual thing: he hit 8 of 10 shots from beyond the three-point line, scored 30 of his 40 points in the second half, and saved the best for last when he nailed a tie-breaking three-pointer with a minute to play to secure the upset, 82-76. The bewildered Zags even double-teamed Steph, but he was too much.

"It was like an opening night, a star performance on Broadway," Davidson coach Bob McKillop told the press corps afterward. "And he was the star, but he had a great cast with him. The audience was sensational. A lot of music, great songs, lots of dancing."

Against Georgetown in the next round, it was *second verse, same as the first.* Playing in Raleigh, just 160 miles from the Davidson campus, the Wildcats were fueled by a partisan crowd eager for an unlikely upset against one of college basketball's elite programs. But the Hoyas kept Steph at bay in the first half and staked out a 16-point lead.

Then in the second half Steph went crazy, scoring 25 of his 30 points, hitting a big 3 and five of six free throws in the last 23 seconds to secure a 74-70 victory.

Could "little Davidson," as some writers called the Wildcats, keep it going against Wisconsin—a nationally ranked 31-4 team—in the Sweet Sixteen?

Why not? This time, the contest wasn't that close. Steph single-handedly outscored the Badgers in the second half—22-20—racking up 33 points on the way to a convincing 73-56 win. It was their *twenty-fifth* in a row, the longest streak in the nation.

Now the Wildcats were the talk of the NCAA tournament, only one game

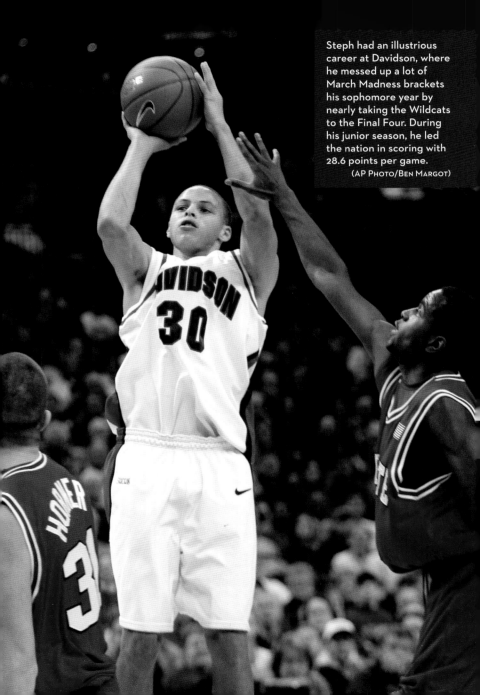

Steph had an illustrious career at Davidson, where he messed up a lot of March Madness brackets his sophomore year by nearly taking the Wildcats to the Final Four. During his junior season, he led the nation in scoring with 28.6 points per game.

(AP PHOTO/BEN MARGOT)

from playing in the Final Four. Standing in the way were the Kansas Jayhawks, the fourth-ranked team in the country with an exceptional 34-3 record.

It was a tight one from start to finish. Steph's three-point shot from downtown with 54 seconds cut Kansas' lead to 59-57. Everyone was thinking, *All Davidson needs is one more three-pointer*. After the Wildcats got a stop, everyone knew who would be taking the final shot of the game—and it would be from beyond the arc.

Steph brought the ball up court with his teammates looking like statues as they waited for Steph to go legend. As the precious seconds ticked off, two Kansas defenders pinned him beyond the three-point line. Four seconds to go. Steph was suffocated; any shot would be an absolute prayer from beyond 25 feet. Just as a third defender rushed him, Steph did the smart thing and dished off to teammate Jason Richardson, who was a good six to eight feet beyond the top of the key. He got the shot off in time, but the ball didn't even draw iron, plunking helplessly off the backboard as the horn sounded.

Little Davidson lost 59-57, and Kansas would go on to win out and capture the NCAA Basketball Championship. But outside Jayhawk Nation, that's not what the 2008 version of March Madness is remembered for. For nine days, March 21 to 30, Steph Curry introduced himself to the basketball fans of America by scoring 40, 30, 33, and 25 points in four games—three upsets and nearly a fourth. The TV cameras couldn't keep their lenses off the peach-fuzzed sophomore or his photogenic parents, Dell and Sonya, cheering him on from behind the Wildcats bench.

Even a member of basketball royalty, LeBron James, had to see for himself what the fuss was about. The Sweet Sixteen game against Wisconsin was played at Ford Field, the Detroit Lions' NFL stadium, and LeBron and the Cavaliers happened to be in town for a game that night against the Pistons. LeBron and a posse of ten made a grand entrance and took their seats behind the Davidson bench. For the 57,000 fans, it was a "wow" moment that had them reaching for their iPhones.

Looking back, I wonder if LeBron felt Steph would one day rival him as the best basketball player in the world.

I doubt it. LeBron isn't wired that way. He's an alpha male who's used to being the top dog because he has been at the pinnacle of the sport for so long.

Steph's personality is different, as illustrated by a story that happened before the start of March Madness, when Steph was named a Wooden Award finalist for the 2007-08 season. His roomie and teammate Steve Rossiter didn't find out until he read a headline on ESPN.com.

"Why didn't you tell me?" he asked Steph. After all, the Wooden Award is a big deal.

Steph gave him a nonchalant shrug of the shoulders and didn't say anything. That was Steph being his usual humble self.

And it looks like that outlook hasn't changed at all.

LAST CALL

Early in Steph's third season with Davidson, he was leading the nation in scoring average with 35 points a game. He had even burned Oklahoma—a strong Division 1 team—with 44 points. That's when Loyola College's coach, Jimmy Patsos, came up with a unique game plan: he decided to put two defenders on Steph every time Davidson had the ball.

What it meant was that every time Steph crossed the half-court line, two Greyhound players swarmed Steph—whether he had the ball or not. It's called a triangle-and-2 defense, which effectively left three players to defend Steph's four teammates when Davidson was on offense.

Remember what I said about Steph's basketball acumen—meaning his IQ on the court? He decided to see how far the Loyola team would take this defense—even to the point of ridiculousness. Would Loyola still put two defenders on Steph if he. . .stood in the corner where the baseline and sideline meet?

Yes, they would. So on each offensive possession, that was what Steph did—stand in the corner and watch his four teammates play against three defenders, kind of like a power play in hockey. His teammates patiently worked the ball closer and closer to the rim, scoring pretty much at will. Since the game was played on Davidson's home court, the Wildcat fans booed lustily as Loyola's coach stuck to his guns—fastening two defenders on Steph while he watched the game unfold from the corner.

Yes, Patsos won the battle: Stephen only shot the ball three times and didn't score a point. But Davidson won the war 78-48, a lopsided margin that matched the number on Steph's jersey.

Patsos was unapologetic for the bizarre coaching decision. "Anybody else ever hold him scoreless?" Patsos asked. "I'm a history major. Are they going to remember that we held him scoreless, or we lost by 30?"

Actually, Coach, we remember that you made a farce of the game.

Davidson wasn't quite as good Steph's junior year, finishing 27–8. Although his point production would drop from the midthirties to 28.6 points per game, that was still good enough to lead the NCAA in scoring. There were also some memorable moments that lit up YouTube and social media, like the time he launched a two-handed 75-foot buzzer-beater to end the first half against Chattanooga. The ball left his hands from the *other* team's three-point line and hit nothing but net.

This time around, Davidson didn't qualify for the NCAA tournament. Relegated to the NIT—the National Invitational Tournament—Davidson lost quietly in the second round to St. Mary's, 80–68. Steph scored 26.

To Go or Not to Go

Right after his junior season ended, Steph had a heart-to-heart talk with his parents. The topic on the table: Should Steph forgo his senior season—and a chance to break the NCAA's all-time career scoring record set by Louisiana State's legendary Pete Maravich—to enter the NBA draft?

Actually, breaking records and taking Davidson to the Final Four weren't uppermost in Steph's mind. If he was going to stay, it would be because he wanted to finish school and earn his college degree.

Dell, who undoubtedly talked to team scouts and heard things through the NBA grapevine, told Steph that he'd likely be a lottery pick, which meant one of the fourteen teams that had missed the playoffs the previous season would draft him. Playing one more year at Davidson wouldn't improve his draft status, and there was the multimillion-dollar risk that he could get injured his senior year and never be the same on the court.

Further complicating his decision was Davidson's policy that requires seniors to take most of their classes on campus. Davidson didn't have summer school, so that was out, as well as taking online courses.

For several days, Steph wrestled and prayed about what to do. One minute he thought he was going to stay for his senior season. The next minute he changed his mind: the prudent move would be to turn pro. For nearly a month, Steph vacillated. In late April, he decided to hold a press conference to announce his decision. But he didn't tell Coach McKillop or his parents what he was planning to do. Dell and Sonya had wisely left the decision up to him.

After sleeping and praying on it some more, Steph woke up the morning of his press conference feeling peace: he would turn pro. Eating an omelet in the school cafeteria with teammate Steve Rossiter, Steph hashed out the positives and negatives one last time. The scales weighed heavier on the NBA side. In his heart, Steph knew he was ready to play professional basketball.

Helping his cause was a burst of height during his three years at Davidson— one inch for each year. He was now 6 feet, 3 inches, following a late growth spurt similar to what his father went through at Virginia Tech.

In announcing his decision to enter the NBA draft, Steph said he would finish his semester classes and then embark on a rigorous workout program. "If you look at my body compared to some point guards and [shooting] guards, I have a lot of work to do," he said. "But if you saw me my freshman year, people were saying, 'Who's this kid in sixth grade walking around in college?' " People weren't saying that now.

Steph noted that he was seven classes short of his degree and would try to finish school sometime down the road. But the NBA could not wait.

"This has been my dream for a long time," he said, "ever since I was a little kid going to my dad's games. I'm at peace with my decision."

Orlando Magic senior vice president Pat Williams said nobody could have predicted that Steph would one day reach the highest heights that basketball has to offer. . .but he has.

(AP Photo/Marcio Jose Sanchez)

TRYING TO TAKE A BITE
OF THE BIG APPLE

When Steph announced that he was making himself available for the 2009 NBA Draft, his declaration set off a flurry of activity in front offices from Portland, Oregon, to Orlando, Florida, where senior vice president Pat Williams took note of the news.

The Orlando Magic had the 27th pick in the first round. "We decided not to spend any time on him," Pat told me. "Not because we didn't want Steph—we did very much—but because we knew he was going to be long gone."

Pat said that all NBA teams were aware of Steph's preternatural abilities, but everyone was aware that he would be scooped up by one of the fourteen teams in the NBA lottery. Since draft day circumstances would dictate when and where he'd get picked, there was intense speculation and much internal debate among NBA executives and coaching staffs about when his number would come up.

Let's face it—selecting college players to join your professional basketball team is a bit of a crap shoot. The road to the NBA is littered with "can't miss" players who flamed out or just weren't good enough to play basketball at its highest level. Steph wasn't one of those "can't miss" players. NBA teams knew he was really good, but they also knew he hadn't fully matured. "To say that anybody predicted that Steph would go to these heights would be stretching the truth," Pat said. "I don't think anybody saw this coming."

Why can't NBA executives and coaching staffs be sure who will make it? It's because no effective tool has been developed to measure the three Ds: desire, drive, and determination. Sure, teams can put players through predraft workouts, interview the players' coaches all the way back to high school, talk to teachers, chat with the parents, and canvass their old neighborhoods. . .but team scouts understand that nearly everyone *wants* to put in a good word for the athletes. "You have to be very alert to what's real and what's exaggerated," Pat said. "It certainly helps to get more than one opinion. You need at least four or five opinions to have a good feeling of certainty."

That was the position the Golden State Warriors found themselves in as draft day, June 25, 2009, approached. The Warriors were coming off a lousy 29–53 season and were in a rebuilding mode. Golden State had the seventh pick in the draft.

Draftniks agreed that Blake Griffin, known for his thunderous dunks while playing for the University of Oklahoma, would go No. 1, swooped up by the Los Angeles Clippers. What happened next was anybody's guess.

Because Steph was such a superior shooter, few teams saw him as a point guard—even though he had handled that playmaking position in his final college season. Some scouts, however, noticing that nearly 60 percent of his total attempts as a freshman were from *beyond* the three-point line, worried about his shot selection. The percentage lessened with each succeeding year, but in his junior season, 48.9 percent of Steph's shots were three-point attempts. Okay, he liked the long ball. Could he hit the 15-footer in traffic?

Height was another concern. At the NBA Draft Combine, he was measured at 6 feet, 2 inches. (Steph's probably a bit over 6 feet, 2 inches but is "rounded up" and officially listed at 6 feet, 3 inches.)

Stevan Petrovic, writing for nbadraft.net, had this predraft assessment:

> He's extremely small for the NBA shooting guard position, and it will likely keep him from becoming much of a defender at the next level. . .can overshoot and rush into shots from time to time. . .makes some silly mistakes at the PG position. . .needs to add some muscles to his upper body, but appears as though he'll always be skinny.

The "strengths" part of Petrovic's scouting report on Steph was twice as long, however. Excerpts included these tidbits: "puts a lot of pressure on defense with scoring ability and quickness". . ."looks fearless on the floor". . ."can get any shot he wants". . ."has great shot efficiency". . ."possesses a great will to win."

In the lead-up to the draft, one NBA general manager projected how things would unfold and determined that Stephen would be the seventh player taken—and Golden State had the seventh pick. That general manager was Steve Kerr of the Phoenix Suns.

Perhaps Kerr saw a bit of himself in Stephen Curry. During a fifteen-year NBA career, Kerr—like Steph, "listed" at 6 feet, 3 inches—made his bones as a three-point shooter during the Chicago Bull's glory years with Michael Jordan. A year younger than Dell Curry, Kerr retired in 2003 with the highest career three-point shooting percentage—45.4 percent—of any player in the history of the NBA.

The Suns had the 14th pick, so there was no way Steph would still be on the board by then. Kerr picked up the phone and called Larry Riley, his counterpart at Golden State. *Let's make a deal. . .we'll give you Amar'e Stoudemire and you give us your No. 7 pick, but we also want you to throw in center Andris Biedrins, forward Brandan Wright, and guard Marco Belinelli.*

Amar'e Stoudemire was a stud, a 6-foot, 10-inch presence in the paint and four-time NBA All-Star. One guy like him could turn the Warriors' fortunes around.

Riley was intrigued. Whether he made a verbal commitment to make the trade is subject to debate, but here's what we know. On draft day, the Minnesota Timberwolves acquired the No. 5 pick in a trade with the Washington Wizards and chose point guard Ricky Rubio, a Spanish player. Then Minnesota, which also had the No. 6 pick, chose *another* point guard, Jonny Flynn.

You may be wondering why Minnesota took *two* point guards when Steph was available. The answer is that Team Curry informed Minnesota that he didn't want to play there. Golden State also got the word not to take him. In fact, *all* the teams ahead of Minnesota and Golden State received a message from Steph's agent, Jeff Austin at Octagon, that Steph wanted to be drafted by the New York Knicks with the No. 8 pick, so they should stand down. That's why Austin told the Warriors and these other teams that Steph wouldn't make himself available for a predraft workout—and many teams won't draft a player unless he works out for them.

Here's what Austin said to Warriors GM Larry Riley: "Larry, I like you a lot and respect you a lot, but don't take Steph. This is not the right place for him. We want him in New York."

Riley also got an earful from Steph's father. "Dell was the same way," Riley would say later. "He was almost cold."

Dell didn't hide his feelings in an interview with the *New York Times*. "The Warriors had some questionable characters on their team, the Knicks really needed a point guard, and we felt that Stephen would fit perfectly with a coach like Mike D'Antoni, playing that fast, up-and-down style. He loved the idea of playing at Madison Square Garden."

With all that drama swirling in the background, the 2009 draft unfolded. When Golden State was on the clock for the No. 7 pick, Riley didn't care how Team Curry felt—they were taking the Baby-Faced Assassin. He was too good to pass up.

Two draft rooms exploded in cheers—one in Oakland and another in Phoenix. Steve Kerr thought he had bagged Stephen Curry. The Suns had a trade deal with Golden State, right?

Not so fast, said Riley. *We didn't expect Stephen Curry to be available, so we're keeping him.*

Things got squirrelly after that. Dell said, "We had no idea that they had agreed to a trade. Obviously, they couldn't put that out. I remember Steve Kerr calling me [the following morning] and saying, 'Don't go to the press conference. We have a trade that they reneged on.' I'm like, 'That's between you guys. We're going wherever they tell us. We can't *not* go.' "

High-stakes poker on both sides. Obviously, we know that Golden State felt like they had a winning hand and stayed the course. The team wasn't about to let go of Steph.

More than seven years later, it's funny how things worked out. But then again, we know that in all things God works for the good of those who love Him and who have been called according to His purpose.

Romans 8:28, right?

THE ROOKIE YEAR

Steph got some good news after he was introduced to the media as a first-round draft choice: his one and only number—30—was available. With that out of the way, Steph readied himself to play professional basketball.

Other good news included the fact that shooting the three-point shot from a longer distance in the NBA wouldn't be much of an adjustment for Steph. He was already accustomed to shooting from "NBA territory," as college basketball announcers liked to say.

The NBA line is three feet longer than the college line at 23 feet, 9 inches. The extra distance didn't faze Steph because he often shot the ball three to five feet beyond the college three-point stripe anyway. In the corners, the NBA line is only 22 feet, which is why you see players pitching a tent and camping there.

Steph had had to adjust to different three-point distances for most of his college career. When he started playing at Davidson, the college three-point line was 19 feet, 9 inches. That explains why he took 60 percent of his shots from beyond the stripe his freshman year. Heck, a 20-footer was catnip to him.

However, for Steph's final college season in 2008–09, the NCAA rules committee scooted the three-point line back one full foot to 20 feet, 9 inches. Did that impact Steph's accuracy? Apparently so. In his sophomore year, the last season for the 19-foot, 9-inch line, Steph made 43.9 percent of his three-point attempts, but dipped to 38.7 percent during his final season of college ball.

Why the decline? I think it's because Steph was called upon to carry the offensive load his junior year, when the team just wasn't as good. He also had the green light from Bob McKillop to shoot from anywhere he wanted. This is when Steph first "extended" the court by taking shots well beyond the three-point line.

Shooting from so far out was a huge change for the game, I daresay even a radical change. Ever since the three-point line was introduced in the 1986–87 season (the year after Dell's final season at Virginia Tech), coaches instructed their players to toe the line when taking the three-point shot—they believed a player's chance of making the shot increased when he was closer to the rim. Steph shot that theory out of the sky by showing he was just as accurate when firing a 25-footer, only steps away from the team bench.

Since long-distance shooting punched his ticket to the NBA, Steph practiced his stroke diligently, putting in work in the gym to prepare for his rookie season. Whatever misgivings he and the family had about Steph playing in Oakland were set aside. *You control only what you can control* was the mantra. Golden State was his team, and it was up to him to make the most of his opportunity. Having grown up in the NBA, Steph knew what was expected of him.

In my estimation, the most fascinating thing Steph did during his rookie season happened *off* the court. Before his first game, he agreed to keep a diary of his year for *GQ Magazine*, a men's fashion publication. His entries would be posted online at the gq.com website.

I have to hand it to Steph: this wasn't a "one-and-done" writing assignment. He must have been paid by the word because he wrote twenty-seven columns by my count—and he didn't stint on the verbiage. Steph's postings are well written (I suspect he had some editing help) and are filled with interesting and unexpected details.

Here's an excerpt from his first post, written shortly after playing his first game in the NBA:

> *On my way to the stadium, I panicked a little because I didn't realize there'd be so much traffic. I had a set time that I was supposed to be at the arena to start warming up.*
>
> *Normally it takes about 10 minutes to get to the stadium, but with the traffic I was a little stressed. I ended up getting there on time, and there was a film crew from NBA.com that wanted to document my first opening night. They wanted video footage of me pulling into the parking lot through to when the game started, but they didn't know when I'd be arriving.*
>
> *So when I got to the arena, I walked all the way to the locker room, and when they came in, they were like, "Agh, we missed your entrance! Can you go back to the car and do it again?" So I went out and pulled the car back in, hopped out, and walked back to the arena again so they could film it. I was down on the court 30 minutes later for my warm-up. I thought I'd be nervous the whole time, but it felt pretty natural. . . .*
>
> *My teammates were basically telling me, "This is what it's all about. This is what we worked so hard for during training camp. For Opening Night." They told me to have fun, to get my feet wet.*
>
> *It's funny: I'm the second-youngest guy on the team, but*

the youngest guy has already played a year. I'm the only rookie. So I was, I suppose, the most excited. I couldn't sit in the locker room. I was jumping up and down, doing extra stretches for no reason. I was the most wired guy in there.

And all the veterans were looking at me like, "This guy doesn't know we have 82 games? It's a long season." I expected Coach to say something to me, but he said absolutely nothing different than he did before the preseason games. So I took that to mean that he knew I was ready to play.

"Coach" was Don Nelson, the second-winningest coach in NBA history and in his fourth year with the Warriors. With a helmet of gray hair and a Boston Celtics pedigree as one of the game's greatest sixth men, Nelson had a reputation as a "mad scientist" who liked to experiment with different lineups when his teams were overmatched—which was the case in Oakland during Steph's rookie year.

Steph earned a starter role, and in the course of playing 80 games, averaged 36 minutes and scored 17.5 points per game—so Golden State was a good place for him to learn the ropes. The highlight of a woeful 26–56 season was making Nelson the NBA's winningest coach ever with a late-season victory against the Minnesota Timberwolves. Thanks to a big effort from Steph—27 points, 14 assists, 8 rebounds, and a career-high 7 steals—the team had something to celebrate in the locker room, showering Nelson's gray mane with Sprite and Mountain Dew.

In between, Steph's first year could be chalked up as a learning experience. He learned that he belonged in the NBA. He learned what it was like playing a long NBA schedule (he appeared in all but two games). His body learned to deal with the dreaded "back-to-back" road games on consecutive nights in different cities.

He also learned to coexist with Monta Ellis.

WEEDING OUT

I don't know if Monta Ellis—a 6-foot, 3-inch shooting guard drafted out of *high school* by the Warriors—was one of those "questionable characters" that Dell referred to before the NBA Draft, but I have a feeling he was. It's evident that Ellis and Steph mixed like oil and water in the Golden State backcourt.

Here's the conventional wisdom on Monta Ellis, as articulated by Howard Beck, an NBA.com senior writer: "Ellis had assumed the aura of a prototypical gunner—his shot count high, his accuracy low, his judgment questionable, his conscience undetectable. Selfish. A bad teammate."

Ellis and Steph got off on the wrong foot from day one of training camp. At a press conference, Ellis was asked about playing with the rookie. "Us together? No. . .can't. We just can't. . .just can't. . . . They [the Warriors management and Coach Nelson] say we can win? Yeah, they say it. But we can't. I just want to win. That's not going to win that way."

Steph was put in an awkward spot, especially after it appeared Ellis wasn't putting his heart into making things work with his new teammate. Ellis was playing for himself, as evidenced by how he hogged the ball and passed only with the greatest reluctance. It was all about him in the offensive forecourt.

During Steph's rookie year, Ellis led the team in scoring with 25.5 points per game. But did it really matter as all those losses piled up?

Team Curry could be excused for having this thought cross their minds: *What if Steph was playing in Madison Square Garden for the Knicks?*

But that wasn't happening. The reality was that Steph and Ellis were the two starting guards on a dreadful, going-nowhere team.

The situation would eventually be rectified, as I'll describe shortly, but until then, Steph had to learn how perseverance would develop his character. And as the apostle Paul described in Romans 5:3–4, with character comes hope.

The first step toward resolution happened in the summer of 2010, when team owner Chris Cohan sold the team to Joe Lacob, the managing partner at a private equity firm called Kleiner Perkins, and Peter Guber, chairman of Mandalay Entertainment. The price of $450 million was the most ever paid for an NBA franchise at the time.

The new owners put their stamp on the team by unveiling new uniforms with a new color scheme and a logo that incorporated a silhouette of the Eastern Span of the Bay Bridge. Lacob and Guber sent Don Nelson packing and elevated assistant Keith Smart as his successor at head coach. Soon, a major trade exchanged three players for All-Star forward/center David Lee of the Knicks.

Lacob also said yes to signing a rookie undrafted free agent named Jeremy Lin, which turned out to be a popular move for a team situated within the nation's highest concentration of Asian-Americans. Lin was familiar to Lacob because the new owner had coached his own son's youth basketball team in the Bay Area, against Jeremy's team back when he was a pip-squeak.

The Warriors improved to 36–46 for the 2010–11 season. Steph matched that modest improvement by averaging 18.6 points a game, but he played fewer minutes—33.6 minutes per game after averaging 38.9 minutes during the final four months of his rookie season. Coach Smart, however, because he felt Steph committed too many ill-timed turnovers, benched him during fourth-quarter crunch time in favor of journeyman backup Acie Law. Smart's decision deprived Steph of much-needed experience taking care of the ball—and closing out games.

There's another reason that Steph's sophomore season wasn't a banner one. During the first month of the 2010–11 season, Steph rolled his right ankle three times. After sitting out several games to rest it, he returned wearing protective but restrictive metal braces on his ankles. In the middle of a road game against Toronto, Steph yanked off the contraptions because he didn't like the way they felt. Another ankle roll in December left him so dejected that he asked reporters if he could skip the usual postgame interviews—the first time he ever asked for that consideration.

In all, Steph would miss eight games during his second season. When the schedule came to a close, he would undergo surgery to rebuild two badly damaged ligaments in his right ankle. A long road of rehabbing lay ahead.

The only 2010–11 highlight for Steph was winning the NBA Sportsmanship Award—known as the Joe Dumars Trophy—given annually to the player who reflects the ideals of ethical behavior, fair play, and integrity on the court. What was really cool about the sportsmanship award was that the winner was determined by a vote of the players.

FALLING IN LOVE

When Steph attended the Central Church of God in his teen years, he met a cute girl in the youth group. Ayesha Alexander was a year younger than Steph and just gorgeous. With a mixed-race background—on her Twitter account, she said her mom has Jamaican and Chinese ancestry and her father's heritage was Polish and African-American—she certainly caught Steph's eye with her exotic beauty and winsome personality.

Both sets of parents saw the looks that Steph and Ayesha were giving each other and knew something was going on, but they never let on. When the kids learned they had a Canadian connection—Ayesha had been born in Toronto and spent part of her childhood there—well, the stars were lining up, right? They even liked the same Canadian candy. (I was hoping they were talking about the Yorkie chocolate bar that's sold in Canuck Country, but alas, they had a mutual sweet tooth for Maynard's Fuzzy Peaches.)

The two hung out during high school but didn't date because Ayesha wasn't allowed to. But Steph didn't have a whole lot of time for a girlfriend, anyway, since he was pretty focused on basketball. After high school, Ayesha moved to Los Angeles to pursue an acting career.

In the summer of 2008, before his junior year at Davidson, Steph was invited to the ESPY Awards show in Los Angeles. He remembered that Ayesha had moved out West and sent her a Facebook message, asking to see her.

"She tried to play me off, saying we could hang out another time if I ever came back in town," Steph said. "She didn't know I was coming back the next week."

The pair spent their first official date walking down Hollywood Boulevard, posing for pictures with a Marilyn Monroe statue and drinking chai tea lattes. You could say they stayed in touch after that, as Ayesha moved back to Charlotte in 2008. She landed a role on *Whittaker Bay*, a short-lived drama series filmed in Wilmington, North Carolina. Ayesha also appeared in one episode of *Hannah Montana* and several small indie movies.

She and Steph officially started dating during his "Elite 8" year at Davidson. Their love grew, and both knew they were headed to the altar. Before the start of the 2010-11 season, Ayesha held a housewarming party at her apartment in Charlotte. This is what happened next, according to a feature story in the *Charlotte Observer*:

> "We were going to go to his sister's volleyball game and then come back here. He showed up dressed really nice, with a fresh haircut and cool sunglasses; I was like, 'Wow,

look at you!'" she says.

After the game, they stopped at Stephen's parents' house to grab the board game Pokeno. As they were walking up the driveway, Stephen stopped. "He asked me if I knew where we were standing. It was the spot where we had our first kiss," she says. "He pulled me close and started saying all these sweet things and then dropped down on one knee. I was in a state of shock."

"She looked at the ring and asked if it was real," Stephen laughs. "The next thing I knew, people were screaming from inside the house. All of our family was inside waiting. It was awesome!"

The handsome couple was married July 30, 2011, at Central Church of God, where they had met and grown up. The bride wore a taffeta, drop-waist Amsale gown with a long, custom-made veil. The groom wore an understated gray suit.

Perhaps the hardest part of the wedding was the start of the honeymoon—those seventeen hours in the air between Charlotte and the tropical paradise of Bora Bora in the South Pacific. But I'm sure the long flight was mitigated by lie-flat seats in first class—they could easily afford the upgrade.

Steph and Ayesha moved into a permanent home they purchased in Weddington, sixteen miles south of downtown Charlotte, and decided they'd rent in downtown San Francisco once the season started—*if* there was a season. A month before their wedding, NBA owners announced they were locking out the players because of a dispute over the collective bargaining agreement (CBA).

With time on his hands, Stephen returned to Davidson that fall to take three classes toward his sociology degree while Ayesha worked toward an online business degree. Perhaps she'd open some type of store in the Myers Park, Ballantyne, or SouthPark neighborhoods.

That was the plan—and then Ayesha got pregnant two months after the honeymoon in late October.

To be named as the Most Valuable Player in the NBA is a special honor. Stephen reached that pinnacle when he received his first MVP award during the 2015 playoff run to the NBA title.

(AP Photo/Jeff Chiu)

5

BREAKING OUT

The 2011–12 season, Steph's third in the NBA, wasn't anything to write home about. I already described in the Introduction how bedeviling ankle issues forced him to miss the last 40 games of a lockout-shortened 66-game season. The only good news was that Steph would no longer have to share the ball with Monta Ellis—the Warriors organization traded the MVP of the All-Gunners team to the Milwaukee Bucks on March 13, 2012. Taking his place at shooting guard was a lanky 6-foot, 7-inch rookie out of Washington State named Klay Thompson. He and Steph had something in common—Klay also happened to be the son of a former NBA player, Mychal Thompson.

Six weeks after Ellis was shipped out, Steph's right ankle still hadn't healed. He had severely sprained the troublesome ankle five times in the 26 games he played after the 2011–12 season began at Christmastime. Since the ankle wasn't responding as well as anyone hoped, Team Curry knew that Steph's NBA career was at risk.

Steph decided to go under the knife. On April 25, 2012, at the Southern California Orthopedic Institute in Van Nuys, a Los Angeles suburb, orthopedic surgeon Dr. Richard Ferkel didn't know what he'd find when he inserted a small high-definition camera into Steph's ankle. If the ligaments were stretched apart like a rotting sweater, he'd have to rebuild the ligaments using tendons from a cadaver. This worst-case scenario came with no guarantees that Steph would ever be 100 percent again, or any kind of force in the NBA.

While Steph's parents and a pregnant Ayesha gathered in prayer in the waiting room, Dr. Ferkel discovered inflamed tissue, bone spurs, and chips of cartilage. Steph's ankle ligaments were a mess, too, but Dr. Ferkel believed a good cleanup would spare Steph from the necessity of having a pair of "used" tendons surgically inserted into their place. Dr. Ferkel vacuumed up the junk in his ankle, performed a few nips and tucks, and closed up the incision. In post-op, the surgeon told Steph the good news and predicted he would need three to four months to recover.

A few months later, in July 2012, Steph was working out with his personal trainer, Brandon Payne. Progress was slow—too slow.

"I feel like I've been doing nothing but rehabbing for two years," said the frustrated basketball player. "I feel like I'm never going to be able to play again."

Steph was getting mopey, but then something good happened that gave him some perspective: he became a father. Ayesha, surrounded by loving family in Charlotte, gave birth to Riley Elizabeth Curry on July 19, 2012.

Life goes on, right?

Steph worked hard in the gym to prepare his ankle (and the rest of his body) for the rigors of an NBA season. He knew this was his chance to shine—the Warriors organization had gotten rid of Monta Ellis and another malcontent, Stephen Jackson. Fresh blood came in the form of the top two draft picks: Harrison Barnes and Draymond Green. A 7-foot center, Andrew Bogut, was acquired by trade.

Steph had a lot going for him. I mentioned earlier how the Warriors signed Steph to a four-year, $44 million contract extension just before the 2012–13 season. It was a gamble for the team, but the Warriors' decision provided financial security for the Curry family. At age twenty-four, with his close-cropped hair and smooth cheeks, Steph still looked incredibly young. At California Pizza Kitchen, one of his favorite haunts, he could count on being carded when he ordered a beer with his pizza.

From the 2012–13 season, Steph grabbed the reins of leadership and didn't let go, running the offense like it was his personal fiefdom. He took three-point shots whenever and from wherever he wanted—just like he had done at Davidson. He tightened up his defense so that he wasn't a liability on the court. Steph played like he had something to prove.

The breakout game in what many call his breakout year was at Madison Square Garden against the Knicks. On February 27, 2013, Steph delivered one of the greatest shooting performances in NBA history. How about 11-for-13 from beyond the three-point arc? That was good for 33 points. How about 7-for-15 from inside the arc? That was good for another 14 points. And how about 7-for-7 from the free throw line? Add 'em all up, and Steph scored 54 points in the

Garden, setting an NBA record for points scored in a game while making ten or more three-point shots.

"He's cooking with hot grease now!" cried out the ESPN play-by-play announcer after Steph swished another rainbow. "Making it rain in New York!"

If Steph's long, three-point shots looked like they rose almost to the Garden's rafters, it's because they indeed had a higher trajectory than other players'. Stats LLC, which tracks shot heights in every NBA arena, determined that the average three-point attempt in the NBA reached a maximum height of 15.77 feet. Steph's three-point attempts were rising to 16.23 feet. The higher arc of his shot meant the rim was more "accessible" when the ball fell toward the basket. Most of Steph's shots entered the rim at an angle of at least 45 degrees—the optimal angle, according to shooting gurus around the league.

Though Steph torched a very good team with all those long-distance shots, the Warriors came up on the short end of a 109–105 score. His highlight reel of three-point bombs, however, was played and replayed on ESPN and other sports shows, introducing him to millions of new fans.

What stands out to me about Steph's breakout season is how he decided to let the ball fly from beyond the three-point line. It was like he figured he had just as good a chance of making the three as he did a two-point basket inside the line. And there is some statistical truth to that supposition: going into the 2012–13 season, Steph made 48 percent of his two-point shots and 44 percent of three-point tries, which isn't a big difference. Since a three-point shot earns 50 percent more points, Steph must have felt that the reward-versus-risk differential was worth it.

Keep in mind that Steph *liked* taking the three-point shot because he generally got a better look at the basket. . .he had more separation from his defender since he was often camped beyond the stripe, waiting for a pass or working his crossover dribble to tie up his defender's legs in knots. Then he would have a wide-open view of the rim.

SHOOTING THE TREY

During Steph's breakout year, he broke out the three-point shot in a big way compared to his first three NBA seasons, when he attempted 380, 342, and

121 treys. (The reason he took so few long bombs in his third year was because ankle injuries limited him to 26 games.)

For the 2012–13 season, Steph launched 600 attempts from beyond the three-point line, making a record-setting 272, which allowed him to slip past Ray Allen's previous high of 269. Steph set the new record despite attempting 53 fewer three-pointers than Allen did during the 2005–06 season. Of his 600 long-range attempts, Steph swished an incredible 45.3 percent.

Steph's 600 attempts led the NBA in 2012–13, followed by Ryan Anderson of the New Orleans Hornets at 557 and fellow Warrior Klay Thompson at 526, the latter connecting on 40 percent. With Steph and Klay attempting so many shots from downtown—and with so many three-point additions to the scoreboard (they made a combined 483, the most ever by an NBA duo)—Warriors.com writer Brian Witt on December 21, 2012, tweeted a nickname that he thought described their long-range exploits: the "Splash Brothers."

Witt said he played off the old Oakland Athletics' nickname for Mark McGwire and Jose Canseco: the "Bash Brothers." The clever basketball version took about as long as a 24-second clock to go viral and stick with the public. No doubt the word *splash* provided a great visual of Steph's and Klay's shots passing through the hoop so perfectly that the net "splashed" back up through the rim.

The Splash Brothers carried the Warriors into the Promised Land—the NBA playoffs—for the first time in six years and only the second time in the previous 18 seasons. The Warriors finished with a 47–35 record, good for sixth in the NBA Western Conference. The top eight teams in each NBA conference qualify for the playoffs.

Golden State's success unfolded with the remarkable cooperation of Steph's balky right ankle. He had no major issues in 2012–13, playing in 78 of 82 games and finishing seventh in the league in minutes played. He upped his scoring to 22.9 points per game (almost a 50 percent increase from his 14.7 point average the previous season), also good for seventh in the league. And Steph connected on 90 percent of his free throws—only Kevin Durant was better at 90.5 percent.

In the first round of the playoffs, Golden State was pitted against the No. 3 team, the Denver Nuggets. When the Warriors took an unexpected 3–1 lead in the series, the Nuggets decided their best chance to win was to get "physical" with Steph, doing anything they could to throw him off his rhythm. Kenneth Faried, a 6-foot, 8-inch forward, impersonated a hockey goon, giving Steph a forearm shiver here and a shove there. But Faried's play was especially egregious when he stuck out his right leg and tripped Steph as he cut down the lane in Game 5. Say what you want, but the strategy worked—Steph scored just 15 points on 7-19 shooting, only 1-for-6 with the three-pointer. The Warriors lost.

Afterward, Warriors head coach Mark Jackson accused Denver of playing "dirty basketball," saying the Nuggets "tried to send hit men" at Steph. Nonetheless, Golden State got revenge by closing out the Nuggets at home to take the series and advance to the next round against the San Antonio Spurs, who had finished the season with a 58-24 record.

The Spurs, one of the NBA's elite teams, were led by Tim Duncan and Tony Parker. Steph and the Warriors played tough but lost the series 4-2. The Spurs would reach the NBA Finals only to fall to the LeBron-led Miami Heat in a seven-game thriller.

For the Warriors, though, the future was bullish. The front office, bolstered by former Los Angeles Lakers great Jerry West as an executive board member and team consultant, was building the team around Steph. "Splash Brother" Klay Thompson was coming into his own. Draymond Green didn't play much, but he was working hard to improve his game and poised to become a huge star. A new general manager, Bob Myers, would trade for Andre Iguodala, known as "Iggy," who would become a key player in taking the Warriors to the NBA championship.

As the 2013–14 season loomed, a lot was coming together for Steph, both on and off the court—including a new shoe deal that turned out to be a perfect fit.

Steph contorts his body to make a reverse lay-in against Cleveland Cavaliers forward Kevin Love. The great players always make the difficult moves look easy.
(AP Photo/Ron Schwane)

6

FROM AIR JORDANS
TO CURRY ONES

Young Steph grew up playing in different basketball shoes, including Reebok, because at one time his father had a shoe contract with Reebok.

Going into high school, Steph wore Nikes. They had street cred, and he got all the free pairs he wanted from his godfather, Greg Brink, Nike's chief financial officer for North America at their headquarters in Beaverton, Oregon. Greg and Dell had become close buds when they were teammates at Virginia Tech.

When Greg and his family would visit the Curry clan in Charlotte, it was like Christmas morning. Greg came bearing gifts in the form of Nike swag: basketball shoes, shorts, workout clothes, T-shirts, training outfits, you name it. Steph and his siblings squealed with delight as they ripped into the packaging.

During Stephen's senior year at Charlotte Christian, Coach Shonn Brown outfitted the entire team in Nikes. It was the same story at Davidson: the Wildcats were a Nike school since the basketball program had negotiated a deal to sport the swoosh.

So when Stephen was drafted by Golden State, he was a Nike guy on and off the court. Like many young men in their early twenties, Steph wore basketball sneakers everywhere—so he needed a lot of different pairs to color-coordinate his outfits with his shoes.

"When I moved out [to Oakland], my mom and dad came to help me get settled into my apartment," Stephen wrote in a "rookie diary" for GQ magazine. "We had to figure out how to get all my shoes over here. That was a little stressful. Playing basketball all my life, I've collected a lot of different basketball shoes. It's pretty much all I wear."

I can only imagine how many pairs of sneakers Steph brought with him to California. Was it twenty? Forty? Fifty or more?

It had to be a lot.

On court during his rookie year, Stephen wore Nike Hyperdunks in Warriors royal blue and California golden yellow with an upper Flywire panel. He remained a Nike foot soldier for the next few years, collecting a modest endorsement check, but after his breakthrough 2012–13 season—when the basketball world collectively nodded its head and said, *That Steph Curry could be the next big thing*—the time was right to strike a big-money shoe deal. Since his current contract with Nike was up, the timing was good.

Shoe deals are *huge* for NBA basketball players. Not only do they establish a pecking order—*My shoe deal is bigger than your shoe deal*—but they can also provide the lion's share of a player's off-court income. For example, LeBron James is riding a lifetime deal that pays him $30 million a year plus a share in shoe sales, a nice bump above the $24 million he received from the Cavaliers during the 2015–16 season.

Kevin Durant sweeps up more than $28.5 million a year for his signature "KD" shoes, which is considerably more than the $20.1 million he was paid in Oklahoma City. Kobe Bryant received $15 million for wearing the Kobe 11 during his final season in 2015–16 while cashing $23.5 million in salary checks from the Lakers. Kobe will continue to receive $15 million a year from Nike through 2019.

The player—ex-player, actually—who tops them all is Michael Jordan, the hypercompetitive Chicago Bulls star who was the face of the NBA throughout the 1980s and '90s. Nearly fifteen years after retirement, Michael Jordan remains Nike's top pitchman, making $100 million a year selling Air Jordans. That contributes to his net worth of $1 billion, according to *Forbes* magazine. (If you've ever wondered how Michael Jordan can afford to own the Charlotte Hornets, a team worth $750 million today, now you know.)

Conventional wisdom says that his Air Jordans changed the sneaker business forever. Before MJ came along, most basketball shoes were boring white—but the bold black-and-red styling of the first Air Jordans screamed for attention. Today, it's hard to imagine basketball players running up and down the floor in "kicks" that aren't a kaleidoscope of colors.

Another notable change is how Michael Jordan single-handedly turned Nike from an ordinary running shoe company into a global powerhouse, the largest and arguably most iconic sportswear brand in the world. Believe it or not,

Reebok was the king of sneaker sales in the early 1980s, targeting women who dance-stepped in aerobics classes. Nike's stock was plummeting because the jogging craze of the 1970s had slowed to a crawl, and the company's fortunes were so bad that it had to close one of its New England factories.

Looking for a way to reinvent the company, Sonny Vaccaro, Nike's talent scout, said there was a charismatic 6-foot, 6-inch jumping jack coming out of the University of North Carolina at Chapel Hill, a player capable of taking off from the free throw line—with tongue hanging out—and gliding through the air for a flying jam. Jordan's fresh face and tremendous personality could reinvigorate the brand, Vaccaro said. Just a few problems: Jordan wore Converse in college, was a self-proclaimed "Adidas nut," and didn't like Nike shoes.

Nike solved all three problems, presumably by adding another zero to the endorsement contract and sweetening the "points"—the percentage of royalty that MJ would receive for each pair of Air Jordans sold. This was one of his greatest spin moves.

As for Steph Curry, there's a story to be told about his negotiations for a new shoe contract in the summer of 2013. Just as he had been a late bloomer on the basketball court, he could one day zoom past his peers wearing sneakers from Under Armour.

SIGNATURE SHOES

You know that Steph grew up hanging around NBA locker rooms. You can figure that he heard his father's teammates chatting about their shoe deals as they killed time before games. Some probably bragged about how much they were getting paid, while others offered opinions on how their sneakers performed or stood up to NBA game conditions. I'm sure they busted each other's chops about how snazzy their shoes looked in comparison to the next guy.

Image may not be everything, but if a player's sneakers aren't flashy or cutting-edge enough, he can get blistered on social media. This is an area where shoe manufacturers constantly try to anticipate the market by designing the hottest-looking shoes and creating a buzz that makes their new model the must-have thing for kids and NBA wannabes. Maybe you aren't Michael Jordan, but you can pretend you are, wearing your Air Jordans and emulating his signature shimmy shake—a hesitation half whirl—on the basketball court.

The hottest sneakers belong to the small number of players who wear their own signature shoes—shoes bearing their own name. At last count, only ten players have their own signature shoe with a US-based brand, while another ten have signature shoe deals with Chinese companies like Anta, Peak, and Li-Ning.

Then there are fifty players who wear PE ("player exclusive") shoes. That means an existing signature shoe from another player has been customized with color or the addition of a unique phrase or personal logo. The Jordan Melo 12 with the Knicks' Carmelo Anthony is an example of a PE shoe.

Even if you're not a franchise player, meriting a signature or PE shoe deal, you're still going to earn a nice check from an endorsement deal with one of the sneaker brands. Nearly all NBA players sign such a merch (short for *merchandise*) deal, earning anywhere from $100,000 to $1 million a year, depending on visibility.

It's been proven that signing up NBA players to wear your shoes drives sales like LeBron driving the lane. The athletic shoe "space" is a $14 billion industry in the United States, so there's a lot of money on the table. Nike dominates that market like Shaq dominates the paint, accounting for 95 percent of all basketball sneakers sold, according to *Forbes* magazine. That's why Nike has no problem locking up three-fourths of all NBA players to shoe deals.

In the summer of 2013, when Steph was a free agent for a new shoe deal, plenty of companies wanted to get their proverbial foot in the door, but Nike got the first shot. After all, Steph had been playing in Nikes going on eight years—he was used to the fit, and he felt comfortable with what his Nikes could do on the court. Steph's ankle issues weren't from a design flaw in his shoes but from the stress he put on the right ankle when making those wicked cuts on the floor.

A pitch meeting was scheduled for August in a conference room at the Oakland Marriott, three levels below the Warriors' practice facility. "I was with them [Nike] for years," Steph told ESPN writer Ethan Strauss. "It's kind of a weird process being pitched by the company you're already with. There were some familiar faces in there."

One familiar face was missing, however—that of Lynn Merritt, a Nike power broker who was also LeBron's brand manager. If Merritt wasn't there to discuss how LeBron and Steph could coexist in the same stable, didn't that signal that King James was Nike's show pony?

Nico Harrison, Nike's sports marketing director, ran the meeting. Steph showed up with Dell, which was a good move—having a father who'd also played in the NBA would be helpful for the advice he could lend, and "many advisers bring success," according to Proverbs 15:22 (NLT).

Steph and Dell leaned back in their chairs, listening to a presentation that ESPN's Ethan Strauss described as "something hastily thrown together by a hungover college student." Here's what happened next:

> The pitch meeting, according to Steph's father Dell. . .kicked off with one Nike official accidentally addressing Stephen as "Steph-on," the moniker, of course, of Steve Urkel's alter ego in Family Matters. "I heard some people pronounce his name wrong before," says Dell Curry. "I wasn't surprised. I was surprised that I didn't get a correction."
>
> It got worse from there. A PowerPoint slide featured Kevin Durant's name, presumably left on by accident, presumably residue from repurposed materials. "I stopped paying attention after that," Dell says. Though Dell resolved to "keep a poker face" throughout the entirety of the pitch, the decision to leave Nike was in the works.

Like a *Survivor* alliance, Steph and Dell got the sense that they were at the bottom of a group that included LeBron James, Kevin Durant, and Kobe Bryant. Steph would never become Nike's premier signature athlete—with all the marketing dollars that come with that status—if he was part of the second tier.

But where could Steph go? Adidas or Reebok? One of the big Chinese sportswear companies seeking a splash in the NBA?

Under Armour had been flying under the radar the entire time. Known for producing sleek workout gear that redefined the modern sports apparel market, Under Armour branched out into shoes in 2006, when it introduced a line of football cleats. A strong response allowed Under Armour to expand its cleat business to baseball, softball, and lacrosse in the late 2000s. But in 2013, Under Armour had yet to sign any of the top NBA players—and even getting players at the end of the bench to wear UA shoes was a challenge. To get *their* foot in the door, Under Armour had begun giving away tons of "merch" to rookies or undrafted free agents who hadn't made a team but *could* one day play in the NBA.

One of those NBA rookies was Kent Bazemore, a 6-5 swingman out of Old Dominion University who averaged four minutes of playing time for Golden State during the 2012–13 season. Since Bazemore was so low on the NBA totem pole, the Nikes and Reeboks of the shoe world weren't showering him with money. But Under Armour took a flyer on Bazemore by sending him product—nineteen big boxes that filled his bachelor apartment.

Bazemore had so much Under Armour gear that he didn't know what to do with it all. Steph saw Bazemore sitting next to stacks of UA boxes in front of his locker; the rookie had received sixty pairs of shoes and dozens of Under Armour shirts and shorts. Bazemore gave away a lot of his freebies to Golden State staffers, which made him a popular guy.

Throughout his first season, the rookie regularly stayed in the gym after practice to work on his shooting. Guess who was the other player polishing his shooting stroke after everyone else had headed to the showers? Steph Curry.

The two men, both of whom had grown up in North Carolina, became friends during these postpractice shootarounds. One time, Steph mentioned that his deal with Nike was up.

Bazemore didn't have a shoe deal but told Steph that he sure appreciated the love from Under Armour. *You need to check out UA.* . . .

And that's how the seed was planted for an American sportswear company with an underdog story that rivals Stephen's. It all started for Under Armour back in 1995, when Kevin Plank, a twenty-three-year-old special teams captain on the University of Maryland football team, was frustrated with how sweat-soaked, heavy cotton T-shirts stuck to his skin underneath his pads. There had to be something better, he thought.

He heard about an innovative fabric technology in which synthetic polyester microfibers with a water-resistant coating could "wick away" moisture from the body and speed up the evaporation process. After graduating from Maryland, he drove to New York's garment district and ordered sample T-shirts made with this new technology. Plank shared the tight-fitting shirts with his old football buddies, who told him they loved how his 0039 Compression T-shirts kept them cool, dry, and light.

The cutest thing ever is Riley Curry, who was three years old when she accompanied her father to the Kids' Choice Sports at UCLA's Pauley Pavilion during the summer of 2015. Riley has sat on Steph's lap during post-game press conferences and sometimes steals the show.

(HELGA ESTEB/SHUTTERSTOCK.COM)

That was all the encouragement Plank needed. He maxed out his credit cards to raise $40,000 in seed money, which he used to set up a company in the basement of his grandmother's row house in Georgetown. At first, he sold moisture-wicking T-shirts out of his car trunk and gave away others to Maryland teammates and friends who'd gone to the NFL. It was all about getting a word-of-mouth buzz going.

A big break came when Plank scored his first big sale to Georgia Tech and he worked out a product placement deal with Warner Brothers for the 1999 football film *Any Given Sunday*. Director Oliver Stone outfitted the players in Under Armour apparel.

The company exploded during the 2000s, leapfrogging sportswear companies like Adidas and Reebok for the number-two spot in the United States behind Nike, which still stood head and shoulders above the competition like a 7-foot, 8-inch center. With $1.8 billion in revenue in 2012, Under Armour was *way* behind Nike's $24 billion.

If Under Armour was ever going to challenge Nike, the company needed a presence in the NBA. The concept had been proven with the introduction of Air Jordans: the endorsement of the very best professional basketball players drove shoe sales, and shoe sales drove shirt sales, and so on and so on.

The year 2013 represented the perfect storm in shoe marketing: not only was Steph a free agent for a new shoe deal, but Under Armour was hungry to land a top player for its fledgling basketball shoe line.

Under Armour had a different vision when seeking athletes to endorse their products. Since Plank's own story was an underdog-to-champion tale, that's the kind of player he wanted to work with. According to company executive Matt Mirchin, "young, underdog, and next" were the key attributes that Under Armour targeted with its athlete endorsers. Steph fit the bill to a T.

By the time the Under Armour marketing and product development teams presented to Steph and Dell, they had done their homework. UA's people knew Steph had ankle issues, and while no one was blaming Nike, they had worked on several customizations they thought would help Steph stay healthy on the court. Then they listened when Steph said he wanted more input on what went into his signature shoes. He indicated he felt like he hadn't been heard by the folks at Nike.

Under Armour stepped up with a deal that would pay Steph a bit less than $4 million a year. But there was plenty of upside—wink-wink—if a Curry signature shoe took off. Steph would be the biggest fish in Under Armour's smaller pond, not swimming among the sharks in Nike's ocean.

So it was decision time. Steph and his family flew to Los Angeles to meet at the Hermosa Beach home of agent Jeff Austin. On the coffee table were sneakers from three companies: Nike, Adidas, and Under Armour. Steph was bouncing his daughter, Riley, on his knee. She was around fourteen months old at the time.

"Which shoes do you like, Riley?" Steph asked.

He was just playing around. But then Riley did the most amazing thing: She got off Steph's knee and walked to the coffee table, where she reached for one of the Nike shoes, inspected it, and dropped it to the floor. Then the toddler picked up a second shoe, from Adidas—and that shoe fell to the floor as well.

That left the Under Armour shoes. Riley grasped one and carried it over to her father. "I knew right then," Steph said.

It's a cute story, but I seriously doubt that was *the* reason Steph and his family made a joint decision to go with Under Armour. But Riley's actions that day certainly confirmed the direction they should go.

Nike, however, had the right of first refusal, meaning it could match Under Armour's offer and keep Steph in the Nike fold.

There was the sound of crickets. Nike let the deadline pass, so Steph became part of the Under Armour team. A rumor circulated on social media that Nike let Steph go because he insisted on having "Philippians 4:13" stamped on the tongue of the sneaker, with the underside reading "I can do all things." But that doesn't sound true to me, and my online search yielded no supporting evidence.

In February 2015, after a sixteen-month development process, Under Armour released the Curry One shoe with a retail price of $120. There *was* a "4:13" scripted on a lace loop and "I can do all things"—the first half of Philippians 4:13—printed inside the tongue, so it's clear that Under Armour allowed Steph to have some input. Naturally, one of the first questions Steph was asked at the shoe-launch press conference was what "4:13" meant.

"It represents a Bible verse I wear on my shoe," Curry told the media. "Philippians 4:13. It says, 'I can do all things through Christ who strengthens me.' It's also my mantra, how I get up for games and why I play the way I do."

Promotional materials for the Curry One shoe came with the tagline "Charged by Belief," another reference to how Steph's faith supercharges his game. The Curry One, each with an "SC30" logo, came in "home" and "away" versions: the former in white with Warrior royal blue and California yellow trim; the latter featuring a black upper with taxi accents and camouflage print. There were also other "color way" editions: "The Underdog," "Candy Reign," and "Father to Son," each telling a unique story that represented Stephen as a husband, father, son, and game changer on the court. Under Armour produced both high-top and low versions.

The spring of 2015 was a good time to launch Steph's first signature shoe since he was leading the Warriors to improbable heights—including the team's first NBA championship in forty years. Sales of the Curry One were incredible, which came as no surprise to anyone in the shoe industry. According to analysts at Morgan Stanley, sales jumped *754 percent*, pushing Under Armour into second place in the shoe market behind only Nike (of course). Under Armour sold a record $153 million in Curry One shoes in the second quarter of 2015, when Golden State was on its title march.

We have no way of knowing if Steph's agent, Jeff Austin, coughed and said "ahem" or if Jeff Plank and Under Armour took the first step, but that $4 million-a-year deal was not going to cut it. In September 2015, both sides announced an "extension" deal that included Steph receiving equity in Under Armour—in other words, a piece of the billion-dollar company.

In exchange, Steph agreed to endorse Under Armour through the 2024 season. The exact terms weren't released, but I would imagine that his agent used LeBron's and KD's contracts as measuring sticks and negotiated upward from there. Although we can't say for sure now, Steph could end up having the biggest, richest shoe deal ever.

Steph's Curry Two shoes were released before the start of the 2015-16 season, at the same time his contract was extended but also right on the heels, so to speak, of the Curry Ones, which had been unveiled eight months earlier. The Curry Twos were updated with seamless heel construction and no sock liner for improved fit—two tweaks requested by Steph.

With the griddle hot, Under Armour filed for several trademarks associated with Steph:

- "Baby-Faced Assassin"
- "The League's Most Unguardable Player"
- "Slay Your Next Giant"
- "Charged by Belief"

At the time of the contract extension, Steph returned to Charlotte Christian, where he supplied thirteen members of the boys' varsity team and its coaches with a pair of "Providence Road" shoes, inspired in part by Steph's time at Charlotte Christian. The shoe's colors—blue, red, and white—were Charlotte Christian's school colors when Steph was in high school. A North Carolina flag is sewn inside the shoe's tongue, and "704"—Charlotte's traditional area code—appears on the lace loop, where "4:13" used to be.

At a school assembly—that had to be fun for the students!—Steph told the young scholars who packed the school's gym that day, "These are my Charlotte Christian-inspired shoes that I am very, very proud of. This is something that brings it all home. I'm able to share my story with not only people that watch basketball but anyone that comes in contact with these shoes."

What an interesting culture we live in. By pointing down to his shoes, Steph is pointing people up toward Christ.

That's typical Steph, always mindful of being a role model, knowing the entire time that role models need spiritual nourishment, too.

Although Steph skipped the 2016 Summer Olympics in Rio de Janeiro to fully rest his sore ankles, he has played for Team USA in the past. In September 2014, he participated in the FIBA World Cup competition held in Barcelona, Spain.

(Natursports/Shutterstock.com)

ON HIS KNEES AND ON HIS GUARD

Life in the NBA can be all-consuming, and its players live in a bubble. But occasionally the outside world intrudes in ways that make even the most jaded player sit up and take notice.

One of those moments happened during Steph's breakout season. On the morning of December 14, 2012, a sick individual named Adam Lanza, twenty years old, walked into Sandy Hook Elementary School in Connecticut and fatally shot twenty-six people—twenty children between the ages of six and seven along with six adult staff members—in the deadliest mass shooting in history at a US high school or grade school. (This massacre of innocent children was the second-deadliest school shooting, after the 2007 tragedy at Virginia Tech, Dell and Sonya's alma mater.)

There's no doubt that December 14, 2012, a Friday, was a dark day in American history. That evening, the Golden State Warriors were in Orlando for a road game against the Magic. The interconference matchup was one of eleven games on the NBA schedule that evening and would be the only time Golden State, a West Coast team, played in Orlando that season.

Many basketball fans are unaware that a chapel service is held one hour before every NBA game—regular season and playoffs—and that players from *both* teams are welcome to attend.

This open invitation makes pro basketball different from other major sports, where players from opposing teams are kept separate during chapel services. NFL players have the option of attending a chapel service—just for their team— on the night before their games. (All NFL teams stay in a team hotel the night before a game whether they are home or away.) Major League baseball chapels are held in each team's locker room on Sunday mornings. Ditto for NHL players.

It's different in the NBA. One hour before tip-off, players from each team are invited to a usable space near the home and visitor locker rooms, perhaps an extra locker room or even the dressing room of the team mascot. Attendance is voluntary.

The home-team chaplain greets the players, and a song may be sung a cappella. The chaplain then speaks for ten or fifteen minutes, sharing scripture and teaching from the Bible. Topics range from overcoming life's challenges to a reprise of the Gospel message, but the basic goal is to equip the players to live lives that glorify God and to encourage them to remain strong in the face of temptation.

The temptations are many, as I'll get into later.

On this particular evening, Jeff Ryan, a local pastor and the Magic chaplain for thirteen seasons, had a heavy heart. The Sandy Hook tragedy weighed on his mind as he prepared to receive the players in an auxiliary room inside the bowels of the Amway Center.

At the appointed time, Jeff was surprised to see the entire Golden State Warriors team, led by head coach Mark Jackson, file into the room. Around eight or nine of the Magic players were there, too. Normally, only a handful of players from each team show up for pregame chapel, but this night featured nearly a full house.

Being in chapel was nothing new for Steph—he attended *every* one, rain or shine. So did teammates like Draymond Green, David Lee, Richard Jefferson, and Jarrett Jack. Of the fourteen players on the Golden State roster, around ten were regulars for chapel.

Jackson, who moonlighted as the copastor of True Love Worship Center with his wife, Desiree, a former R&B singer, underscored the importance of attending chapel. He wasn't in the pulpit as often as he liked since his church was located in Van Nuys in Southern California. But in Orlando on December 14, 2012, he asked the entire team to join him for the service because of what had happened at Sandy Hook.

Jeff Ryan didn't look at the players as NBA professionals that evening. Instead, he saw them as young men—kids playing a game—who weren't that far removed from college or even high school. Some of them were young dads like Steph, the father of a six-month-old girl.

That evening, Jeff did something he'd never done before as the Magic chaplain. "Guys," he said, "I'd like to start by asking everyone to get on their knees."

The somber players, many incredibly tall, got out of their fold-up chairs and knelt on the thin carpet covering the concrete floor. Speaking without notes, Jeff said:

> You know guys, you may have heard about the tragedy that happened today up in Sandy Hook. From what we know, there were a lot of kids who lost their lives and a lot of parents who are still scrambling to understand if their kids are hurt or even dead. I want you to know that entire community will never be the same.
>
> They've been impacted with tragedy that makes no sense. There will be no way to explain this other than, "It is evil." If you didn't believe that evil is real before this, evil is real today.
>
> For those who know God through Jesus Christ, as horrible and horrific as this day is, we know there's hope. We know there's hope that only Jesus can bring these families. We know there's hope in the comfort of the presence of Jesus, and we know that there's hope in the power of His name.
>
> This is not the end. Evil wanted it to be the end, but it's not the end because we know that Jesus overcame death. And so today, our hearts are broken. Our community is shattered. Parents are deep in pain and anguish that none of us could ever understand.
>
> So let us go out and play with the gift that God has given us to impact others, that they would see our hope is not in what we do, but our hope is in Jesus Christ. Let us lift up and pray for those in Sandy Hook for the days and the weeks and the years to come, and that God will use this moment, as painful as it will be.
>
> The Bible tells us that God works in all situations for His good. We don't know how, but we know that God will work somehow in this tragedy.

And then Jeff asked everyone to bow their heads and close their eyes as he closed in prayer:

> *Dear Lord, we thank You that we can be on our knees. Sadly, Lord, it's a place that tragedy most often drives us. But Lord, it should be a place where we reside. Lord, our pants should have holes, and our knees should hurt because we're on them so much praying to You and praising You.*
>
> *So Lord, we surrender as we kneel today. We know that people look to us sometimes in the midst of tragedy. May they find us looking to You for hope in the midst of this tragedy. Thank You, Lord, that everyone is willing to humble themselves before You today, almighty God.*
>
> *We know You are God, You are holy, and You are sovereign. So Father, we thank You and we ask Your blessing on those in Sandy Hook, that they would be comforted by Your love. We ask this in the name of Jesus Christ, amen.*

Wasn't that an amazing message? And just as noteworthy was that thirty minutes later, five players from each team approached the midcourt circle for the opening tip-off. The referee tossed the ball in the air and those players played hard—one of the beauties of sport.

"As much as these guys are competitors, they realize that there are only four hundred or so professional basketball players in the NBA," Jeff said. "Playing is a privilege, not a birthright. They worked hard to get into that room. They know they are paid to perform, and they are going to play hard."

Steph did his part in Orlando that night, leading all scorers with 25 points, but the Warriors fell behind early and lost 99–85.

TAKING SECURITY UP A NOTCH

Also attending that day's chapel service in Orlando was Ralph Walker, the Warriors' director of team security.

Ralph, an African-American in his late fifties, had been hired the previous year after he retired from the Oakland Police Department. There, he was part of the downtown foot patrol, reaching out to the homeless and keeping an eye on drug dealers.

Part of his twenty-six years on the force was spent running the Police Activities League in East Oakland, one of the roughest neighborhoods in the East Bay. From a worn-out middle school gym, he organized basketball leagues for boys from eight to eighteen and coached and mentored kids in after-school programs.

Ralph could handle himself well on the basketball court, so he won instant respect there. Coming out of high school, Ralph had been good enough to play ball at St. Mary's College in nearby Moraga; after college, he was drafted in the fifth round by the Phoenix Suns. Although he never played in the NBA, he was known as "Ralph the Rocket" because of his 41-inch vertical leap.

By the time the Warriors hired him in 2011, due to his vast law enforcement experience, Ralph knew how to handle a crowd and size up potential threats. Both capabilities would be important to his role in NBA security.

Ralph's job was to protect players from fans and from themselves—especially the threat coming from women on the prowl. I'm talking about groupies who flock to airports, hotel lobbies, restaurants, and sports arenas whenever the team goes on the road. These women hang out wherever they can catch the eye of the players.

I gained insight into the sexual temptations players must deal with when I wrote a cover story for *Focus on the Family* magazine on Los Angeles Lakers star A. C. Green, who compiled two impressive streaks while suiting up for sixteen seasons in the NBA:

1. Playing in 1,192 consecutive games, the most ever by an NBA player.

2. Remaining a virgin until he married at the age of thirty-eight, after his NBA career was over.

"Iron Man" meets the "Iron Virgin."

"I don't know how many virgins there are in the NBA, but you can probably count them on one hand," A. C. told me. (I thought he was probably being generous with his estimation.) "Some of my teammates threatened to set me up with women who would make themselves available to me, to see how strong

I really was," he said.

Attractive ladies can weaken any player's resolve to stay pure. They dress provocatively and give the players "come hither" gazes that leave nothing to the imagination. Some of the women, unfortunately, are looking to get pregnant by an NBA player. They see having an NBA star's child out of wedlock as a fast-track ticket to child-support payments that begin in the five figures and can rise to sums of $75,000 a *month*. The number of NBA players who father children outside of marriage is staggering, and their child-support payments are often their biggest monthly expense.

"Remember, the players are targeted," explained Jeff Ryan, the Magic chaplain. "Some handle it well, and some don't. Unfortunately, there are plenty of guys who get caught up in the women thing and get their heads turned. They come into the league with the best of intentions, wanting to be faithful, wanting to be strong, but they give in to temptation."

That's one reason teams hire security personnel—because as big and strong as these talented players are *on* the basketball court, they must be even stronger *off*. If their cell phone numbers get out, they receive shockingly explicit photos. They're left messages at the hotels and on social media. I would venture to say that we have no idea how far some women are willing to go to "meet" a star player like Steph.

Ralph Walker understands that, which is why he will go to any length to protect Steph. Not because Steph doesn't possess the right moral compass, but because someone whose face is so recognizable needs someone at his shoulder when he's out in the public. *Everyone* wants something from Steph—an autograph, a fist bump, eye contact, or an exchange of hellos. Some females are more nefarious, offering something he doesn't want to accept.

Quite frankly, because of the dangerous world we live in, Steph also needs physical protection. I'm sure measures have been taken in that department as well. There are simply crazy people out there. From the cloak of anonymity the Internet provides, people write online about how they're "gonna kill" Steph if he hits another three-point shot or tweet that they'll slash him the next time he steps onto an NBA court.

Scary stuff.

That's why, when Steph became a household name during the championship

Steph loves to drive the lane, draw defenders, and pass to the open man. He's averaged 6.9 assists per game in his seven seasons in the NBA.

(AP Photo/Darren Abate)

season of 2014–15, general manager Bob Myers prudently decided to dedicate Ralph Walker solely to Steph, hiring a second security person for the rest of the team.

These days, Ralph is Steph's shadow from the time he arrives at the players' parking lot at Oracle Arena and walks from his car to the players' entrance. Once inside, Ralph is never more than a step or two away from Steph—and he sticks close to the bench during warm-up and game time. When Warriors coach Steve Kerr calls for a time-out, you'll notice that Ralph comes out of nowhere to hover around Steph during the break in the action. Dressed in a suit and tie, sporting short black hair and a thin goatee flecked with gray, Ralph Walker does have a presence about him. Perhaps that's because he's the only person who can guard Steph Curry.

If the Warriors are on the road, Ralph sticks to his man from the time he steps off the team plane until they board the flight home. If Steph wants a Jamba Juice in the middle of the afternoon, Ralph walks him to the store. If Steph wants to go see a movie, Ralph sits next to him. But the director of security draws the line when Steph sits down for a meal at a restaurant. Even if Steph invites him to have a seat—part of Steph's "Southern hospitality" breeding—Ralph declines, instead choosing a table between the superstar and the front door.

At team hotels, fans are sometimes kept at bay outside; sometimes they linger in the lobby, hoping to get Steph's autograph. Ralph calls them "snipers" because more than a few are trying to "ambush" players for signatures, which they can later sell for profit.

Personally, I don't see how Steph's autograph can net much because he's signed *so many* throughout his basketball career. He's known as one of the most generous signers in any sport. Klay Thompson, his teammate, is another player who signs willingly. "Even if we pull into a city at 2 a.m. on the road, Steph and Klay are gonna sign," Ralph told *Sports Illustrated* writer Chris Ballard.

I wouldn't be surprised if Steph signs at least 50 autographs a day, either for fans or for merchandise and memorabilia. If you figure that happens 200 days a year, he's signing a minimum of 10,000 autographs a year. Since Steph's been signing autographs since his Davidson days—maybe even back to high school because of his precocious talent and having a dad playing in the NBA—I wouldn't be surprised if he's nearing the 100,000 lifetime mark.

When Steph signs before and after games, he often uses a Sharpie that was handed to him for the first autograph. One of Ralph's responsibilities is to return the Sharpie to its rightful owner. All in a day's work for an important job that starts the moment Steph leaves his hotel room and continues until he returns, well after midnight.

Following road games, when Steph retires to his hotel room, Ralph finally bids him good-bye—then keeps an eye on the hallways. He stays on the same floor as Steph—and probably sleeps with one eye open. The Warriors also hire additional outside security to patrol the team floors in their hotels.

None of this goes unnoticed by Steph. To give you an idea of how important Ralph Walker is to him, I refer you to Steph's MVP acceptance speech in May 2015, when he had this to say:

> Where's Ralph Walker at? Where's Ralph? He's guarding the door [laughing]. Ralph, our head of security, I've seen a lot of you the last three years. You're at every event, every practice, every game. You're our eyes when we don't have them, and we appreciate you putting yourself out there anytime we need you being there for us.

The British have a term for what Ralph does—he's a *minder*, someone whose job is to look after someone. But he's more than that. . .he provides accountability. I imagine that is something of utmost importance to Steph, as well as Ayesha and Steph's family.

You and I have no idea of the fishbowl life that Steph finds himself in. Everywhere he goes, people look at him as if they've seen a ghost. They want a word, an autograph, a selfie with the star.

This is Beatlemania stuff. During the 2016 NBA All-Star Weekend in Toronto, Steph and Ayesha boarded a helicopter that flew over the Canadian city and deposited them on a skyscraper rooftop near Yorkdale Shopping Centre, where he would make an appearance at Foot Locker in support of his Under Armour Curry Two shoes.

I've seen photos of the thousands who jammed the mall, shoulder to shoulder, craning their necks and holding up smartphones for a peek at their basketball hero. Surrounded by a phalanx of security that included Ralph, Steph snaked his way through the massive crowd and did several media interviews. Then he good-naturedly participated in an impromptu three-point shootout with local teens on a basketball rim set up in the middle of the mall. Around it were promotional materials for the "All Star" and "Energy" versions of his signature sneaker.

And then it was time to go. Ralph suggested ducking into a clothing store and popping out the back of the mall, where a car would be waiting. Steph didn't want to disappoint the fans who wanted one last look. He wondered if they could go out the front of the mall instead.

It's your call, Steph.

Here's how Gerald Flores of *Sole Collector* described what happened next:

> As Curry wraps up his allotted media time, the swarm outside the gates grows more restless. "Curry! Curry! Curry!" chants start. Followed by an "MVP! MVP! MVP!" chant. . . .
>
> Against the suggestion of security to go through the back tunnel exit, Curry doesn't want to disappoint his fans. He surrounds himself with a human shield of four bodyguards in an attempt to make it through the front gates. The anxiety written on his wife Ayesha's face is palpable.
>
> Steph doesn't even get a foot past the gate before people charge toward him. . . . Curry turns his whip-thin 6' 3" frame around with a facial expression that connoted, "My bad."
>
> Back tunnel exit it is.

Actually, there was no back tunnel. Ralph led Steph and Ayesha to a clothing store. Once inside, they reprised John, Paul, George, and Ringo and hightailed it out the back to escape the mob. Ralph said Steph found it all very exciting.

All in a hard day's night.

Two days later, in a shiny Canadian city where he spent a formative year of his life, Steph held the ball at the half-court line as the last few seconds of the 65th NBA All-Star Game ticked away. On an afternoon when defense took the day off, Steph's West team was ahead 193–173.

Just before the buzzer sounded to end the game, Steph launched a half-court jump shot.

Of course the high-arc shot swished through the net.

AMERICA'S MOST
AWARD-WINNING AIRLINE.

DANGER
DO NOT OPEN DOOR
ED WARNING LIGHT IS FLASHING
(CABIN PRESSURIZED)

Steph exults as he leads the Warriors off the team plane while holding the Larry O'Brien NBA championship trophy on June 17, 2015. The night before, Steph had been instrumental in a Game 6 victory over the Cleveland Cavaliers, which gave Golden State its first NBA crown in forty years. Steph is trailed by center Andrew Bogut after their flight landed at Oakland International Airport with thousands of Dub Nation fans waiting to cheer their heroes.

(AP Photo/Jeff Chiu)

8

A ROUTINE WORTHY
OF BROADWAY

By the start of Steph's fifth year in the NBA, the 2013–14 season, fans and the media noticed that Steph had put together a pregame routine that was equal parts engrossing, entertaining, and educational.

Having a routine. . .if Steph had learned anything from being a professional basketball player, it was that routine provided a sense of structure and familiarity. By doing the same thing over and over again—like taking the three-point shot from a certain spot on the floor and watching the ball sail cleanly through the basket—Steph developed confidence and muscle memory to make that shot without thinking. Great athletes always make it look easy, especially when there's tons of pressure on their shoulders at crunch time.

Steph is a creature of habit. I'm guessing he was the kid who always ate peanut-butter-and-jelly sandwiches for lunch and wouldn't ask for anything else. His way of preparing himself to play a basketball game started long before he reached the NBA, but once he became a professional, certain habits and mannerisms evolved and have stayed with him to this day. For instance, before every home game:

- he listens to the same music on the drive in to Oracle Arena (one of the artists he really likes is Christian rapper Lecrae)

- he always backs his car into his spot in the player's parking lot (he has a fondness for Porsches)

- he waves to the same female parking attendant as he walks into the arena

It's safe to say that Steph has a ton of habits, or what I call rituals—from taking afternoon naps, to eating the same pregame meal (he likes his wife's pasta or a Subway sandwich), to chewing on his mouth guard while he shoots free throws.

One time Steph skipped his pregame nap to see how he would feel. Not a good idea—he felt out of sync during the game. "When you wake up from a nap, you know it's time to get ready and get focused and go to the game," he told the *New York Times*.

In the locker room, Steph dresses as he always does. . .slowly and methodically. He takes a Sharpie to write "I Can Do All Things" or "Romans 8:28" on new basketball shoes. He sends out the same Tweet before every game—"Lock in!"—a reminder for him to focus his energies on the upcoming game and do what he needs to do to help the team win.

The topper to his pregame routine is a twenty-minute exhibition of choreographed drills that starts precisely ninety minutes before opening tip-off. With Ralph Walker running interference, Steph leaves the locker room in game shorts and a gray Warriors T-shirt, doffing an imaginary hat to fans who've come early to witness a series of dribbling, passing, and shooting exercises that warm up his muscles and hone his motor skills for the challenge ahead. He enters the arena with his shoelaces untied, however, preferring to tie them once he hits the floor.

"It's amazing how many fans come to the building to watch him warm up," said Pat Williams of the Orlando Magic. "It's like how fans used to show up early at Fenway Park to watch Ted Williams take batting practice. It's the same with Steph. They want to see him go through his warm-up routine, and they want to watch him shoot. It's a beautiful thing to watch."

It's also an expensive thing to witness. Fans seeking the experience unwittingly raised the average ticket resale price for 2015–16 Warriors road games to $154, a 40 percent hike from the previous season. (Don't worry. . .you can watch Steph's pregame warm-up routine for free on YouTube or nba.com.)

Steph starts by taking his place on the baseline, facing the opponent's basket. With a basketball in each hand, he hefts both balls in the air so that they touch each other before falling back into his palms. Then he leans over and begins dribbling each ball simultaneously, rat-a-tat style, no more than a foot off the floor. It's like a championship boxer hitting the speed bag. Depending on the rhythm he's attempting to capture, the balls hit the floor at exactly the same instant or intermittently.

Steph says these dribbling drills wake up the feeling in his fingertips. He's so unbelievably adept at dribbling—the balls are an extension of his hands—that I wonder what dribbling legend Marques Haynes of the Harlem Globetrotters would have thought of Steph's virtuoso control.

Then Steph ratchets up the intensity by crossing over and figure-eighting the balls between his legs. The effect is hypnotic because his timing is impeccable. After a minute or so of around-and-through-his-legs dribbling, one ball is discarded. Steph shovels the other one to assistant coach Bruce Fraser, who's about twenty feet away. Fraser slips the ball back to Steph, who dribbles between his legs and flips the ball back to Fraser to start the drill all over again.

Once the pass-and-dribble drill is done, Steph moves to the left side of the basket, about six feet away. He starts tossing underhanded "floaters" toward the backboard with his left hand (Steph is right-handed), watching how the ball spins off the glass backboard and into the basket. These short flips are like golfers practicing tap-in putts.

From there, Steph takes a few steps back to free throw length, where he tosses one-handed shots—again with his left hand—toward the rim. As soon as a shot is in the air, Fraser is bouncing the next ball, so Steph wastes no time letting his next shot fly. It's all about finding a shooting rhythm.

The warm-up shifts to the right side of the key, where Steph attempts a series of one-handed shots with his right hand, usually shooting off one foot to increase the difficulty factor. They're called "leaners." A few steps closer, and Steph flings a few over-the-shoulder hooks at the glass backboard. Then it's on to medium-range jumpers, one after another from the baseline. *Catch and shoot. Catch and shoot. Catch and shoot. . . .*

Every three seconds, Steph ripples the net. He then moves to several other spots on the floor, where he accepts passes from Fraser. He takes a one-bounce dribble between his legs and flings a superhigh lofted shot—so high he'd never take a shot like that under game conditions. Several ultrahigh shots fall out of the rafters and pass through the net.

Next Steph moves to the wings of the court, firing away as fits his fancy from either side of the three-point arc. He works his way clockwise around the key, a shot going up every three to five seconds, around fifteen to twenty shots per minute. The purest shooting stroke in the NBA is on full display for several thousand early birds who've been allowed to move up close for the warm-up session. For these fans, young and old, it's like watching Phil Michelson on the driving range or Bryce Harper in the batting cage.

Then Steph goes long—from the edge of the center circle at half court. These 40- to 43-foot bombs from the team logo don't go in as often, but when they do, they elicit a collective "aahh" from the crowd. Wait—there's more perimeter work to do, followed by a half-dozen shots from the dead corner, the sweet spot for three-point shooters since it's only 22 feet from the rim.

Coach Fraser then "guards" Steph around the key for a series of shots over his outstretched arms. . .some straight-up jumpers, others of the step-back variety. A few free throws (Steph rarely takes more than a handful before games), and he's done.

Except when Steph's home at Oracle Arena. There's one last shot to make, and it's from the "tunnel" between the locker room and the court. The distance has been measured at 52 feet, according to beat writers who note that Steph makes no more than five attempts but usually stops when he swishes one of his two-handed flicks from an impossible distance away.

The "tunnel shot" originated in 2012 when Patrick Sund, the associate general manager of the Warriors, playfully wagered Steph that he couldn't make one from the players' tunnel in three attempts. The stakes: loser had to buy a meal. *I'll take that bet.*

According to the ushering crew, Steph drains his long-range tunnel shots more often than not. Once his last tunnel attempt is in the air, Steph sprints from the tunnel back to the locker room, trailed by Ralph Walker.

Then Steph towels off and gets ready for the best parts of his pregame ritual—hearing a devotional thought and praying at team chapel.

SUDDEN IMPACT

The Warriors improved for the third straight year in the 2013–14 season. Steph kept his head down and turned in his best professional season ever: he had a career high in scoring average with 24.0 points per game, good for seventh in the NBA, and raised his assists to 8.5 per game. He tied for second in the league for the most triple-doubles (at least 10 points, 10 rebounds, and 10 assists in a game). The exclamation point to Steph's season was becoming the first Warrior to start an All-Star game in nineteen years.

Golden State finished 51–31, good for the sixth seed in the NBA Western Conference. A tough Game 7 loss to the Los Angeles Clippers in the first round, however, left a bad taste in the mouth of the person who counted most—team owner Joe Lacob. The ax had to fall, and the sacrificial lamb was head coach Mark Jackson.

Jackson wasn't well liked within the Warriors organization or by the San Francisco media, which viewed him as a Bible thumper—not a good fit for one of the most liberal areas of the country. There were rumblings that Jackson stretched himself thin by flying to his Los Angeles–based church to preach on too many Sunday mornings.

When the season ended with a narrow loss to the Clippers, Steph was asked by Lacob and general manager Bob Myers for his input on Mark Jackson. Steph expressed support, noting that Jackson had taken the Warriors to the playoffs for the previous two years and given the team stability. (Steph had had three coaches during his first three years in the league.)

Lacob and Myers thanked Steph for sharing his thoughts—then fired Jackson anyway. Nine days later, the two team officials announced the hiring of Steve Kerr, who had never coached before in the NBA or at any level. Kerr had stepped down as president and general manager of the Phoenix Suns in June 2010 and become an NBA analyst for the TNT network. Lacob, who had a long relationship with Kerr, signed him to a stunning five-year, $25 million guaranteed deal.

Steph's reaction was succinct: he said the "semi-quick hire" was "kind of a shock" to him and most of his teammates. "There's no sugarcoating it. It was a weird, expedited situation that we didn't see coming," he said. "And guys are human. You have to be able to adjust to it and have some time to respond. That's kind of what happened. I think we'll be fine once we have a clear picture of what's going on next year."

The same day Kerr was hired, *Mercury News* beat reporter Tim Kawakami asked Mark Jackson his thoughts. "Congratulations to him," he replied, referring to Kerr. "Wish him the best. He's inherited a great team with a great future. And they are a championship-caliber team."

STARTING HOT

That coaching pastor could pass for an Old Testament prophet after what happened during the 2014–15 season.

The Warriors started out as the NBA's hottest team ever, winning 21 of their first 23 games on the strength of Steph's breathtaking shooting, tricky ballhandling, and clutch three-point shots with seconds to play. After years of hearing NBA pundits complain that he was too small and not athletic enough to dominate games, Steph was proving night after night that he was head and shoulders better than bigger competition.

He blew the roof off at home, packed arenas around the country, and supplanted LeBron James as the face of the NBA. He shot even better from the three-point line (44.3 percent) than he did from 16-to-23 feet (38.1 percent). Steph sank 286 three-pointers, eclipsing the record he'd set two years earlier. He also had a career high in steals, his second-best year for rebounds, and his best defensive rating to date.

Steph was the quiet yin to the brash yang of Draymond Green, the muscular 6-foot, 7-inch power forward who liked to trash-talk and run through defenses like a bull let loose in a Pottery Barn. Steph always took a more low-key approach, content to launch a three and nonchalantly turn up the court without waiting to see if the ball swished through the net—because he knew it was going in. When the roar of the crowd reached his ears signifying that his shot was good, he tapped his heart and pointed his right index finger to the sky.

The Dubs—as their fan base had taken to calling their team in a truncated pronunciation of the *W* in Warriors—finished the season with a sterling 67–15 record, becoming the tenth NBA team to win that many games. No one was surprised when Steph was named Most Valuable Player during the playoffs.

Golden State's run for a championship didn't lack for anxious moments. In the Western Conference final, Warriors fell behind the Memphis Grizzlies 2–1 but won three straight to capture the series—and propel Steph and Company to the NBA Finals against the Cleveland Cavaliers.

There were several great story lines going into the best-of-seven series, the most obvious being the Steph-versus-LeBron angle. Both were fighting over the same bone—supremacy in the NBA. The head-to-head matchup did have

Steph received his second consecutive NBA Most Valuable Player award from Commissioner Adam Silver during the 2016 NBA basketball playoffs. He also became the first NBA player to win the MVP award unanimously.

(AP Photo/Marcio Jose Sanchez)

a bit of a David-versus-Goliath feel: it was diminutive Steph slingshotting balls from beyond the three-point line versus LeBron's inside game that featured head down, get-out-of-my-way drives to the basket for his rim-rattling dunks.

LeBron could take over a game like few others could—or ever did. As a muscle-bound, 6-foot, 8-incher, he could play small forward or power forward. But the reality is that LeBron played wherever he wanted on offense. He could plant himself in the low post and go to work with his back to the basket, but he preferred to freelance by hanging out in the offensive wings off the key. Once he had the ball, LeBron looked for a clear path to the rim. If he saw daylight, he was gone. If not, he would plow his way past defenders and slam the ball through the hole with a vengeance. No one could stop LeBron—the defenders' only hope was to slow him down and try to make him take an off-balance shot, which he was prone to do.

And there was another important aspect to LeBron James's game: he could collapse the defense around the basket, which allowed him to pass off to an unguarded teammate waiting beyond the three-point line. Teams playing against Cleveland were taking their chances on how good the Cavs' outside shooting was.

The biggest story line, at least from a team standpoint, was that both clubs entered the NBA Finals with long title droughts: the Warriors had last won the NBA championship in 1975, when Rick Barry was making underhanded free throws; the Cavs had never won a championship since the team's inception in 1970–71.

Further adding to the intrigue was the "Cleveland curse," the reality that the Rust Belt city next to Lake Erie hadn't won a major sports championship since the Cleveland Browns captured the NFL crown fifty years earlier in 1964. And then there was the fact that LeBron was Ohio's favorite son, having grown up in nearby Akron and in his second stint with the Cavs after a four-year exodus to Miami. He had picked up two NBA championship rings with the Heat in 2012 and 2013.

When the Cavs captured Game 2 at Oracle Arena and followed that win with another victory in Game 3 on their home court, the Warriors were down 2–1 again. Time to kick things up a notch: Steph provided the offensive firepower and Andre Iguodala supplied the defense against LeBron. The Warriors swept the next three games (including two in Cleveland) to capture Golden State's first championship in forty years.

Dub Nation was on top of the world! When Steph looked at his cell phone after the game, there were 174 congratulatory texts from friends and family.

After clinching the NBA championship in Cleveland, Steph and his teammates, along with his family and buds from his Davidson days, celebrated at Morton's, a steak house adjoining their team hotel in Cleveland. The party started at 1:30 a.m. and the food and drink flowed until dawn.

A time to laugh, and a time to dance, as Ecclesiastes 3 says.

A Family Ring

Besides Steph's promotion of scripture, there were several things that caught my eye about the 2014–15 season. Each revolved around Steph's family.

The first is how often the ABC cameras found Dell and Sonya in the stands. It was nice to see a loving couple praised for the way they raised Steph, as well as for staying together for more than twenty-five years. As a husband and parent myself, that was great to see.

Next, Steph's adorable, not-quite-two-year-old daughter nearly stole the show as she sat on her daddy's lap for his postgame pressers. After Game 1, as Steph walked past the family waiting room toward the interview room, Riley ran after him. "She had that look, like she wasn't going to take no for an answer," Steph said. "So I said, 'All right, come with me.' She sat up there, and that's when her personality shined bright."

The little rascal slipped under the table, prompting Steph to lift the fabric cover. Next thing the reporters knew, Riley was lifting up the cover and playing peekaboo with the press.

"She's got a great sense of humor," Steph said. "Now she's the star of the family. If we go somewhere without her, the first question people ask us is, 'Where's Riley'?"

The last family member I want to mention is Ayesha, who turned plenty of heads on Twitter when she sat next to Dell and Sonya to cheer on her husband. I really liked hearing how she set Twitter ablaze earlier in the season by tapping out the following message:

Everyone's into barely wearing clothes these days huh? Not my style. I like to keep the good stuff covered up for the one who matters.

I've omitted the trio of "bawling" emojis at the end of her Tweet, but from the reaction she engendered, you'd think she just ran over a stray dog. A sampling:

• "Christians love to judge. Some things never change."

• "I knew I didn't want you to speak."

• "A woman dressing the way she wants to doesn't make her a hoe. This freaking thinking is whack as @#$%."

Ayesha had more than her share of defenders with more than 98,000 "Likes" and 71,000 retweets. It's just hard for me to understand why so many people go to the trouble of tapping out snarky comments, mean-spirited retorts, or plain old nasty invectives just because Ayesha said she prefers to dress modestly and let Steph see the "good stuff."

Sheesh. . . .

I have a feeling that Ayesha is a go-getter. Not only is she raising two young girls in their preschool years and trying to maintain a peaceful household in the midst of the Steph maelstrom, she's also a budding entrepreneur.

Back in 2012, she launched a website, ayeshacurry.com, populating it with recipes, posts, and pictures about faith, fitness, and family. She flexes her business muscles by selling Ayesha Curry's Little Lights of Mine Extra Virgin Olive Oil (8.5 ounces for $12) on her website, with 10 percent of the profits going to a charity called No Kid Hungry.

Ayesha's recipes received a lot of hits, and her social media platform grew parallel to Steph's meteoric rise that started in 2013. Her Instagram feed has 3.3 million followers, and her Little Lights of Mine YouTube channel has more than 400,000 subscribers. Her videos are professionally done—would we expect anything less?—and varied. . .there are videos on everything from being a mom to potty training to making homemade bread and Steph's favorite pasta.

Ayesha really branched out in 2016. She partnered with celebrity chef Michael Mina for a "pop-up" restaurant, International Smoke, that came out of Mina's test kitchen in the Marina district of downtown San Francisco. International Smoke opened during the 2016 NBA Finals and closed by Labor Day, serving prix fixe family-style platters of different kinds of barbecued meat with Peruvian purple potato salad, black-eyed peas, and braised mustard greens. Ayesha and Mina got to know each other in February 2016, when he offered her a role as a line chef at his Super Bowl 50 tailgate party at nearby Santa Clara. Mina put Ayesha to work: there were nine hundred invitees.

Who knows. . .maybe Ayesha and Michael Mina will decide that their barbecue restaurant concept is worthy of a million-dollar investment (or whatever it takes to open an eatery in the city). I'm sure having Steph around to sample the entrées would be great for business.

Ayesha has a lot on her plate these days, including two projects scheduled for Fall 2016. One is the release of her first book—*The Seasoned Life: Food, Family, Faith, and the Joy of Eating Well*, published by Little, Brown and Company.

The other project may or may not happen—Ayesha's own cooking show on the Food Network. A pilot, called *At Home with Ayesha*, has been filmed, so check the Food Network or its sister network, the Cooking Channel, for when the show airs.

Amanda Haas, the culinary director for Williams-Sonoma, has been Ayesha's mentor since meeting her in 2013.

"I was blown away by her recipes, her voice, and her strong point of view," Amanda said. "People want to be influenced by Ayesha. Like Stephen, she can be a role model, too. The thing is, we don't have to pick."

Talk about dressing up in his Sunday best. . .here Steph accepts the award for best record-breaking performance at the ESPY Awards at the Microsoft Theater in Los Angeles on July 13, 2016.

(CHRIS PIZZELLO/INVISION/AP PHOTO)

9

"I'LL TAKE STEPH FOR
$400, ALEX"

If you're looking for an indicator that you've become part of pop culture, I would think that having your own category on the *Jeopardy!* game show would rank near the top.

That happened to Steph the night before the 2015–16 NBA season started, when the popular syndicated show unveiled a category called "Steph Curry Dishes" during its Double Jeopardy round. Host Alex Trebek, speaking to the three contestants—Sean, Beth, and Tom—said, "You're going to love the first category. It is 'Steph Curry Dishes.' It helps if you know who Steph Curry is."

The two millennial guys, Sean and Tom, not only knew who Steph was, they easily rattled off all five of the correct "questions" (*Jeopardy!*'s trademark twist) like they were part of Steph's posse. I'll reprise them here, and you can see how you would have scored playing at home. Answers are at the end of the chapter.

Steph Curry Dishes

$400

Steph dishes out thank yous to cafeteria workers who he thinks made a special meal for him in an ad for this network.

$800

When Steph is making an assist, AKA "dropping" this coin, he's dishing it to someone else for the score.

$1,200

If Steph dishes out 10 assists along with 10 points & 10 rebounds in a game, he achieves this coveted feat.

$1,600

One of Steph's best dishes at the 2015 All-Star Game was to this Maverick big man, AKA the Dunking Deutschman.

$2,000

Steph dished & dealt in the NCAA, leading this southern state's Davidson College to the Elite Eight.

Since *Jeopardy!* reminds me of another popular game—Trivial Pursuit—I thought it would be interesting to share other informative nuggets about Steph and his family:

TIME IS ON HIS SIDE

In another example of the Curry zeitgeist, Steph emojis—called StephMoji—were the No. 1 seller in the Apple app store during the 2016 NBA Finals, surpassing reality star Kim Kardashian. The Steph-themed emojis featured him wearing a chef's hat, putting on a green, and sitting at a press conference with daughter Riley.

The real, as opposed to the cartoon, Steph was listed in *Time* magazine as one of its "100 Most Influential People." *Time* asked professional ballerina Misty Copeland to share why Steph deserved inclusion. "I'm in awe every time I see Stephen Curry play," she wrote. "He combines a never-before-seen skill set with the panache and flair of a great performance artist."

It's Steph's "humility and grace," combined with his world-class physical presence, that makes him so special, she said.

I read what Misty Copeland wrote *after* the publisher and I decided the subtitle of *The Right Steph: How Stephen Curry Is Taking the NBA to a New Level—with Humility and Grace.* That's pretty cool.

NO THREE PUTTS, THOUGH

Steph is a golf nut who loves making threes somewhere else besides a basketball court.

He picked up the game from his dad early on—Steph was just eight or nine years old—and he's a real stick, as they say in golf. He was the No. 1 player at Charlotte Christian for three years and played with Dell all the time during the off-season. I've seen video of Steph's golf swing, which is a beautiful motion since he learned to do it right at a young age.

Steph is easily the best golfer in the NBA, playing to a 1 handicap. That means he regularly shoots in the mid-70s and is a near-scratch golfer. He even went low at the famed Pebble Beach, where he signed for a two-under-par 70, a feat that astounds me as much as his basketball ability. I got to play the famous seaside course myself one time and was amazed by how tiny the greens are—which doesn't come across on television. Pebble is one tough course.

Steph and Dell love playing father-son golf and have participated in a bunch of celebrity pro-am tournaments over the years, including their own—the Curry Celebrity Classic. Since 2014, though, Steph hasn't been able to squeeze the eponymous event into his schedule any longer. Their tournament was a fund-raiser for the Ada Jenkins community center in Davidson, North Carolina.

Steph had more time for celebrity golf before the Warriors were a playoff team. In late April 2010, Steph played in the pro-am of the Quail Hollow Championship—the PGA tour stop in Charlotte in early May—with Charlotte police chief Rodney Monroe, NASCAR driver Michael Waltrip, and pro golfer Steve Lowery.

Local golf writers reported that Steph was "uncommonly long" off the tee and made three birdies that day. "It was a lot of fun," Steph said. "I got to measure myself against a tour pro. We had a blast, but I think my dad got me by a couple of shots today."

Knowing that Steph has a jones for golf, I would imagine he tees it up every chance he gets. But with a young family and so many people and opportunities tugging at him, he can't get out as often as he would like. Steph plays out of the California Golf Club in South San Francisco and has competed in the American Century Championship—the biggest and most prestigious celebrity golf tournament, held in July at Edgewood Tahoe Golf Course in Stateline, Nevada.

After winning his first NBA ring in 2015, he looped with President Barack Obama at Martha's Vineyard, carding a 75 to the President's 84. Asked what he and the Leader of the Free World talked about, Steph said, "He opened up a lot about how he never really valued his anonymity until it was gone. That was the biggest thing I got from that conversation 'cause obviously I'm kind of going through that a little bit myself."

A little bit, Steph?

Only a golfer can appreciate the following story. After the Warriors won their NBA championship in Cleveland in June 2015, players ran around the Cavs' home court hugging each other in ecstasy. Golden State's Andre Iguodala, another golf fiend, ran up to Steph with a huge smile and arms outstretched. "We're going to Augusta!" he screamed, like a kid on his way to Disney World.

Steph smiled. He hadn't forgotten what coach Steve Kerr had said to the both of them a couple of months earlier: if the Warriors won the NBA championship, he'd make sure they could play a round at Augusta National, the storied Georgia golf course that's home to the Masters golf tournament. Augusta is private, one of the hardest courses to get on, but if you know the right people. . .well, Kerr knew the right people.

In February 2016, the Warriors faced the Hawks in Atlanta then had a travel day before a game in Miami. On their off day, Steph and Andre—along with Dell, team executive Jerry West, and owner Joe Lacob—played Augusta. What an awesome experience that must have been, walking the fairways of "Amen Corner," taking on the challenge of the iconic, par-3 16th hole, striding up the steep greensward toward the 18th hole and the members' clubhouse, imagining what it would be like to put on a green jacket.

Steph called it a "bucket list" kind of day. He even birdied the first hole—shooting a three—before the golf gods exacted their revenge. "It can only go downhill from there," Steph said. "That's exactly what happened."

And that's golf, as they say.

On a final golf note, Steph has a "bromance" going with Jordan Spieth, the Masters and US Open winner and fellow Under Armour athlete. (They appeared in an Under Armour commercial together, along with Misty Copeland, called "Rule Yourself.")

Jordan—born in 1993 and named after a certain guy who used to play for the Chicago Bulls—met Steph before a road game against the Dallas Mavericks in 2016.

In an Instagram that Steph sent out that day, he said he finally "got to chop it up with #UA family @JordanSpieth. Inspiring guy! We agreed on 5 shots when we get to play this summer. He's definitely shorting me but it's all good."

HE CAN HAVE IT HIS WAY

As a youngster, Steph was not only talented with a basketball, but he was an exceptional child actor, too. I say that after watching his scene-stealing performance in a Burger King commercial that aired in the '90s when he was five or six years old.

The thirty-second spot has tyke-sized Steph tentatively approaching his dad in their living room. "Hey, Dad, how did you get so big?" he asks in a respectful son-to-father tone.

Dell's adjusting his sneakers. "I guess I just grew up that way," he says.

Then Steph asks his dad what it takes to become a basketball player like him. Dell good-naturedly says, "Well, you really gotta want it. You gotta taste it. You gotta be able to smell it. I mean, you really gotta be really hungry for it."

You know where this is going. . . .

"Dad, can we go to Burger King? I am really hungry."

I know. . .a cheesy ad, but the way Steph earnestly and naturally said his lines made the BK Curry campaign a success. (For some reason, I see a cute commercial in Riley's future.)

As for Steph, he's in a ton of TV commercials these days—more than sixty different ad campaigns, according to ispot.tv. He's starred in ads for Chase Bank, Under Armour, Apple iPhone 6s, Brita, State Farm, Taco Bell, NBA Game Time app, Degree Dry Spray, Muscle Milk, Kaiser Permanente, My Brother's Keeper Alliance (with President Obama), PlayStation Heroes, and Kids Foot Locker. My favorite was the lighthearted "This Is SportsCenter" promo where Steph, in a Golden State game jersey and shorts, pushes a tray through the cafeteria line in the ESPN lunchroom.

He trails a couple of SportsCenter anchors, kibitzing about last night's game, when he says, "I had that 27/10 last night" (referring to 27 points and 10 assists), "and today, Chicken Curry" (the dish being served in the ESPN cafeteria for lunch). As he slides his plastic tray along the serving line, he thanks the cafeteria workers for honoring him by serving Chicken Curry every time he has a good game.

DOWN UNDER DOUBLE

Ask Australians what they think of Stephen Curry's latest performance, and they are likely to recall his recurring roles in popular TV drama series such as *The Secret Life of Us* or *The Time of Our Lives*.

The Aussie edition of Stephen Curry is white and twelve years older than our Steph.

MAKE A WISH

Steph's heart for giving isn't an act. I'm confident that his parents taught him the importance of giving to others and tithing to support the local church.

I would imagine that Steph gets requests to support dozens of well-meaning ministries and charities. One of his most visible efforts is his longtime association with Nothing But Nets, a United Nations initiative that protects Third World families from malaria by providing life-saving bed nets. Every time he sinks a three-point shot, Steph donates three bed nets. He traveled to a Tanzanian refugee camp in 2013 to see firsthand how the mosquito bed nets improve and save lives.

Over the years, Steph has met young fans with life-threatening medical conditions who asked to meet him as part of the Make-a-Wish Foundation. If you ever want a lump in your throat, watch any number of YouTube videos showing Steph offering encouragement and taking selfies with these hurting kids.

BROTHERLY LOVE

Steph isn't tall for an NBA player, but he casts a long shadow. A lot of people don't even know that he has a brother playing in the NBA.

Seth is a little more than two years younger than Steph, close enough in age for them to scrimmage against each other and participate in shooting drills organized by Dell when they were growing up.

He and Steph were teammates on the Charlotte Christian basketball team, so I'm fairly confident in stating that opposing teams didn't like seeing *two* Currys in the backcourt. When Big Brother went on to Davidson and led the D-1 Wildcats to the Elite Eight in the NCAA tournament, you'd figure that Little Brother, who was averaging 22 points a game at Charlotte Christian in his senior year, would get a good look by college recruiters.

That didn't happen, so Seth enrolled at Liberty University, a Christian college in Lynchburg, Virginia. He was slightly smaller than Steph, at 6 feet, 2 inches.

Like Steph, he made some waves his freshman year, dropping 26 points on Virginia in a big upset win. He ended the season averaging 20.2 points per game, leading all freshmen nationally.

His getting-stronger-every-game did get Seth that second look. Duke's Coach Mike Krzyzewski—Coach K—took a flyer on him. Seth transferred to Duke, a perennial powerhouse in college basketball, where he acquitted himself well over the course of three seasons. He even led the team in scoring his senior year with 17.5 points per game.

Seth wasn't drafted by the NBA, but the Warriors signed him in the fall of 2013, most likely as a favor to Steph. The Warriors didn't keep Seth long, however, releasing him and making him a free agent. He was then picked up by the Santa Cruz Warriors, the D-League affiliate of Golden State. Over the next two seasons, Seth signed a trio of 10-day contracts with the Toronto Raptors, Memphis Grizzlies, Cleveland Cavaliers, and Phoenix Suns, but he only played a total of 34 minutes of garbage time in two years.

I got to hand it to him: Seth kept plugging away in D-League, playing for Santa Cruz and the Erie (Pennsylvania) BayHawks. He showed that he had Steph's long-range touch, sinking 46.7 percent of three-point attempts for the BayHawks, but wearing the name "Curry" on the back of his jersey held him up to a different standard. It was like he could never measure up to his famous brother.

Then Seth played lights out in the NBA's 2015 Summer League in Las Vegas. Vlade Divac, a 7-foot, 1-inch center who played with Dell Curry in Charlotte in the late 1990s, was sitting in the stands, remembering when eight-year-old Seth would shoot around with Steph before Hornets games. Divac, general manager of the Sacramento Kings, saw the potential in Seth, who averaged 24.3 points per game in Summer League. The Kings needed a three-point shooter.

Divac signed Seth to a contract, and this time he stuck in the NBA. He played in 44 games during the 2015–16 season, averaging 15.7 minutes a game and 6.8 points per game, but what happens from here on out is a jump ball.

"I've heard people say I'm a Curry and that helped me get where I am," Seth said. "Sometimes I think it's the opposite."

SISTER ACT

Steph's little sister, Sydel, joins her parents and Ayesha at all the big playoff games and says she has the laid-back personality of her dad and the competitive energy of her mom. Like Sonya, she's quite a volleyball player.

Sydel is a 5-foot, 9-inch setter at North Carolina's Elon University, due to graduate in 2017. While attending Charlotte Christian, she had a tough choice to make—volleyball or basketball?—because she was talented at both. Overlapping seasons forced her to choose one, so she decided to blaze a path in volleyball.

When she meets recruits or is introduced to someone at Elon, she says, "Hi, I'm Sydel."

"She never says her last name," Elon coach Mary Tendler said. "I'm assuming she does that on purpose because she just wants to be Sydel."

Good for her.

NO BOOKING FEE

When the Warriors make their annual visit to Charlotte, the Hornets' TV analyst never has a problem booking Steph for a pregame interview.

That's because the Hornets' color commentator is Dell Curry. He's been in the Hornets' broadcast booth since 2009 when he came alongside longtime play-by-play announcer Steve Martin for the team's TV broadcasts on Fox Sports Carolinas and SportSouth.

Dell has had a great life since he hung up his sneakers. He got to coach his sons in basketball as a volunteer at Charlotte Christian, and he was there for Steph during his formative years. Once Steph was drafted by Golden State, Dell must have felt the time was right to take the broadcasting gig.

That must be interesting—commentating on a son who is playing against *your* team. "His first year, it was really very difficult because when I watch his games I focus in on him," Dell said. "I caught myself doing that the first time [the Hornets] played the Warriors, and I'm like, *Hey I gotta back up. I gotta watch everybody, watch the game.* But I try to be as equally balanced as I can."

I've heard that Dell can be critical of his famous son's shooting form or dumb turnovers, but everyone knows it's tongue in cheek, part of what's made Dell a popular analyst. During the 2015 NBA Playoffs, the Hornets expanded Dell's role, naming him the franchise's ambassador and special projects adviser in addition to color analyst. The ambassador duties included community programs, charity outings, and fundraising events.

A LEAD BALLOON

Occasionally, people make dumb jokes about Steph. That happened at President Obama's final White House Correspondents' Dinner in April 2016 when Larry Wilmore of *The Nightly Show* on Comedy Central remarked that it made sense that the President was hanging out with Steph "because both of you like raining down bombs on people from long distances."

You could say the joke blew up in Wilmore's face.

CONSTRUCTIVE CRITICISM

Nobody's perfect, and I'm sure Steph isn't either. Maybe he leaves dirty socks on the floor, doesn't clean up after their labradoodle Reza, or forgets to put out a trash can full of dirty diapers when Ayesha asks him to.

We don't know what happens behind closed doors, but there's nowhere to hide on the basketball court. I'm nitpicking here, but NBA superstar Steph can get sloppy on occasion and turn the ball over. Thinking back to the 2016 NBA Playoffs, I can recall more than a few times when he played a little too loose with the ball. Steph forced passes that were picked off, or he whipped around-the-back passes to defenders rather than teammates.

He's also had some listless games where his three-point shot was off. I understand how that can happen, but after five, six, eight misses from downtown, Steph was still launching rainbows from a good five feet beyond the three-point stripe. *Why doesn't he take a couple of shots from closer range, even two-point territory, to get his stroke going?* I'd think.

That's not his mind-set, however. "I don't really worry about the shots that I missed," he said during the 2016 NBA Finals. I would imagine that's the let-'er-rip attitude that the best pure shooter in the NBA has to carry into every game. Steph thinks the best way to beat a shooting slump is to keep shooting. He and fellow Splash Brother Klay Thompson "are allowed to take any shots they want," said Coach Kerr. "That's the rule. Steph and Klay are, nobody else is. I trust their judgment."

So why doesn't Steph make just about every three-point shot in a game the way he does in practice—one after another?

Well, he's always being hounded and manhandled, drawing long-armed defenders who attempt to cloak him like a blanket. But there's also the pressure of the moment. As golfing legend Bobby Jones, founder of Augusta National and the Masters championship, used to say, "There's golf, and there's tournament golf."

In the same way, there's basketball and there are basketball *games*, meaning it's one thing to shoot around with your buddies or join a three-on-three half-court contest, but it's quite another to be part of a five-on-five, full-court NBA game with three referees, announcers and analysts critiquing your every move, 18,000 fans cheering like crazy in the stands, and tens of millions more with their eyes glued to the TV.

Steph has put in the work to shoot with confidence, block out the crowd noise, maintain a steel-minded concentration, and not be overwhelmed by the importance of the situation. So he's going to keep shooting no matter what, figuring the next hot streak is right around the corner.

And that's what makes him great.

He does have one habit that drives my wife, Nicole, crazy. She doesn't like how Steph approaches the free throw line with his mouth guard hanging outside his mouth, gnawing on one end while he casually sinks another free throw. She thinks it looks dumb.

(In a sign of the Apocalypse, one of Steph's used mouth guards hit the auction block after a fan picked it up off the floor at the end of a 2016 game. The mouth guard, marked with the Warriors logo and Steph's name and number, was expected to sell for $10,000 at an auction held before the start of the 2016–17 season. There might be more out there: Steph told late-night host Jimmy Kimmel that he uses a new mouth guard every three to four games.)

Getting back to more mundane matters, I've noticed that Steph can drift into a monotone in postgame interviews. Those on-court interviews can probably get awfully stale after so many years, so it has to be a challenge to come up with something new or interesting to say, moments after an emotional game. On the plus side—and this is huge—I love how Steph usually manages to work in a reference to God or his faith in those postgame interviews.

When he won his first MVP award, he was quite bold:

> *First and foremost, I have to thank my Lord and Savior Jesus Christ for blessing me with the talents to play this game, with the family to support me, day in and day out. I'm His humble servant right now, and I can't say enough how important my faith is to how I play the game and who I am.*

Well said, Steph.

DON'T WRITE THAT CHECK

Speaking of turnovers, Steph has a standing bet. . .well, it's not really a bet. It's a financial and family-minded incentive *not* to make turnovers.

One night several years ago, Sonya watched her son lose the ball—frivolously—way too many times. She asked Dell what was a reasonable number of turnovers per game for an NBA player, and he said that three turnovers was fairly normal.

So Sonya presented her son with a challenge: *If you make more than three turnovers in a game, you pay me $100 a turnover, and if you make less than three turnovers per game, you get to take back $100 from the pot.*

In other words, if Steph commits three turnovers, he doesn't owe her anything; if he commits four turnovers, he puts $100 in the pot; five turnovers cost him $200, and so on. A game against the Phoenix Suns early in the 2014–15 season was painful for his wallet: 10 turnovers cost Steph $700.

The way Steph and Sonya have things worked out is that any "fine money" still in the pot after the season is over is earmarked for Sonya, who treats herself to a shopping trip.

"I like it," Steph said. "I'm a competitor, so I like those kind of challenges. It's a win-win for me. I take care of Mom and I have a lot less turnovers."

ABOUT THOSE TATS. . .

I love that Steph is not tatted up like many NBA players.

It seems like you have to get inked to join the NBA Players Union these days. Tattoos fill fleshy biceps, cover the shoulders, and run up and down the arms, wrists, and legs of many of today's players.

There's actually a website that keeps track of players and their tattoos: nbatattoos.tumblr.com. Sixty percent of the Warriors players have tats, including Steph, who has just a couple visible on his arms.

His most noticeable tattoo is located on the underside of his right wrist. It's a verse from 1 Corinthians 13, the Bible's "Love Chapter," inked in Hebrew even though the apostle Paul originally wrote it in Greek. The Hebrew phrase is *Ahava le'olam lo nichshelet*, which means "Love never fails." Asked if he can repeat the phrase in Hebrew, Steph said, "I can't. I'm working on it."

He has another tattoo on the underside of his left wrist that's like a two-deck headline:

TCC

• 30 •

The TCC comes from a motto passed along by Davidson basketball coach Bob McKillop: "Trust, commitment, and care."

Steph and Ayesha got similar tattoos consisting of two arrows pointing to each other on the inside of their left triceps a few years ago. They have a pregame ritual. . .before the opening tip, Steph looks at his arrow tattoo and taps on it, and she does the same from her seat—or from the living room couch if Steph is on the road and she's at home.

What does the arrow tattoo stand for?

"This signifies that the past is behind us and the future is in front of us, so we stay in the middle, in the moment. I smack my tattoo, and she does the same," he told *Parents* magazine.

Said Ayesha, "It's a reminder for him to have fun. I never want him to forget that."

Steph has one other tattoo that isn't very visible: an italic *A* where his wedding ring would normally be on his ring finger. Due to safety concerns, basketball players aren't allowed to wear jewelry, but he still wanted a reminder of his marriage commitment on his ring finger when he plays. Steph got the tattoo in 2014.

I've seen Steph wearing what looks like a fairly wide and simple silver wedding ring at press conferences. Ayesha has a beautiful diamond ring.

TIPS FOR MARITAL BLISS

Ayesha was asked by *Hello Beautiful* magazine to describe her secrets to a successful marriage. She shared this advice:

- **Be independent.** This stems from her desire not to be viewed as a "basketball wife." I've already mentioned how she has a cookbook in publication and a cooking show in the works.

- **Pray together.** You gotta love hearing this. . .especially because Ayesha says her relationship with Steph is based on their faith in God. "It's the foundation for everything that I do, really," she said. "It's not so much about the religion, it's more about the relationship that I have with God and making sure that I pass that on to my kids. With my relationship with my husband, it's what it's founded on."

- **Communicate.** You have to stay in touch to stay close.

- **Make time for each other.** Sure, it's a cliché, but making time for each other never goes out of style.

GOOD CALL

Steph didn't play for Team USA in the 2016 Summer Olympics in Rio de Janeiro, citing the need to rest his body.

Although it would have been fun seeing him make mincemeat of the shorter international three-point arc, it didn't make sense to put his ankles and knees under more stress after an intense 2015-16 season. A last-week push to secure the NBA record of 73 wins, four rounds of playoffs, and an emotional Game 7 loss to the Cleveland Cavaliers probably took the thrill out of playing in the Olympics.

WHAT BOTHERS HIM?

Steph says his biggest pet peeve is when people sneeze without covering their nose. . .and snakes are his biggest fear.

HE CAN LEVITATE

Yes, Steph can dunk and first threw it down at Davidson as an eighteen-year-old freshman. These days, if he's on a breakaway and ahead of defenders, he's content to lay the ball against the glass. If he feels like he could get caught, and needs to make sure his shot won't get blocked, he'll stuff the ball through the hoop.

Only happens a few times a year, though.

A NEW HOME FOR STEPH?

The Golden State Warriors will move back to downtown San Francisco beginning with the 2019-20 season when the new Chase Center in the Mission Bay district is ready.

That's if all goes as planned. With NIMBY (not in my backyard) forces fighting hammer and tongs against the construction of an 18,000-seat arena, there will inevitably be delays. But the construction of a new arena and return to San Francisco—where the "San Francisco Warriors" played in the Cow Palace in the 1960s before moving to Oakland in 1971—is a grand idea.

During the season, the Currys live in Walnut Creek. The distance to the Chase Center, according to Google Maps, is twenty-five miles. The computer estimates a forty-five minute drive, but that has to be under the most optimal driving conditions. I've found it can take forty-five minutes going two miles in downtown San Francisco.

Will Steph and the family move to San Francisco if the Warriors start playing downtown? I wouldn't think so. The family currently dwells in a Mediterranean-style, 7,894-square-foot estate that came with a gourmet kitchen (good for Ayesha's budding cooking career), billiards room, wine cellar, attached casita (perfect for when Dell and Sonya are in town), and five bedrooms and five bathrooms.

One can never tell what the future may bring, but if Steph is still firing three-point shots for Golden State at the end of the decade, I predict they'll stay in bucolic Walnut Creek—because they'll want the room and the green grass for the kids.

As for his commute, he can have someone drive him. Better yet, why not take a helicopter across the bay? He'd be there in ten minutes.

Steph can certainly afford it, so we'll see what happens.

ANSWERS TO THE *JEOPARDY!* QUESTIONS:

1. What is ESPN?
2. What is a dime?
3. What is a triple-double?
4. Who is Dirk Nowitzki?
5. What is North Carolina?

You won't see Steph dunk very often; he prefers to kiss the ball off the glass on a lay-in. But sometimes if he's in traffic around the rim, he'll go to the rack and throw it down.

(AP PHOTO/MARCIO JOSE SANCHEZ)

10

A SEASON TO REMEMBER,
A GAME 7 TO FORGET

I don't normally pay attention to NBA games in October and November. That's the middle of the college football season and the heart of the NFL schedule, so my DVR tends to record football games (and the World Series) during the autumn months.

Heading into Thanksgiving week of 2015, I saw the news that Steph and his Golden State teammates had gotten off to the fastest start in NBA history, winning their first 16 games to best the previous mark set by the 1948–49 Washington Capitols and the 1993–94 Houston Rockets. Six wins later, the Warriors broke a 131-year-old record for any professional team at the start of the season when they surpassed the 20–0 record set by the 1884 St. Louis Maroons baseball team. (Was there really a pro team called the Maroons? Statisticians had to dig deep to discover that record.)

Now the Warriors were within striking distance of the longest NBA winning streak, set by the 1971–72 Los Angeles Lakers. They'd won 33 consecutive games with Jerry West, Wilt Chamberlain, and Gail Goodrich. I firmly believed the Warriors could best that mark set by the Lakers, but standing in the way was a pair of dreaded "back-to-back" road games.

On Friday, December 11, 2015, the Warriors had to go the extra mile to defeat the Boston Celtics, going double-overtime in the Boston Garden to bag win No. 24. The following night, in Milwaukee, their legs gave out in a decisive 108–95 loss. I guess the Bucks stop here.

If you were cheering on the Warriors, the rest of the 2015–16 season was a lot of fun to watch. Some NBA stars from yesteryear were not so enamored, however; they got their knickers in a twist about how Steph, Klay, Draymond, and Co. were annihilating teams with long-distance shooting and slashing drives to the cup. Hall of Famer Oscar Robertson went on ESPN's *Mike & Mike Show* to say that today's coaches didn't know anything about defense, which gives a shooter like Steph Curry an edge.

Steph "has shot well because of what's going on in basketball today," Robertson said. "When I played years ago, if you shot outside and hit it, the next time I'm going to be on top of you. I'm going to pressure you with three-quarters, half-court defense. But now they don't do that. These coaches do not understand the game of basketball, as far as I'm concerned."

Kareem Abdul-Jabbar, the great Lakers center, and Cedric Ceballos, who played six years for the Phoenix Suns in the 1990s, made similar comments, which created a flurry of discussion. There were also former players who said, *Sure, my team could take the Warriors. What's so special about them?*

Steph was asked to respond on the *Warriors Plus/Minus* podcast by the Bay Area News group. He had this to say:

> *It's starting to get a little annoying just because it's kind of unwarranted from across the board. We have a very competent group, and we have fun when we're out there on the floor, and it shows, obviously.*
>
> *We enjoy what we do. But for the most part, you don't hear us talking about, you know, comparing ourselves to other great teams and "We could beat this team, we're better than this team." We're living in the moment.*

Comparing today's players with stars and teams from decades past makes for an interesting debate, but it's like a dog chasing its own tail. You'll never come to a conclusion.

Dell had the right take when asked about Oscar Robertson's comments. "I don't think you can compare the '90s, the '80s, the '70s to what's happening today," he said. "Different players, different rules, different game. Those comments he made...I think they were funny. I didn't put a lot of stock in them. That's all I'll say."

Still, I did appreciate how a couple of writers—Bob Ryan of the *Boston Globe* and Scott Ostler with the *San Francisco Chronicle*—wrote thoughtful pieces in the spring of 2016 comparing Steph with Pete Maravich, basketball's enigmatic icon of the late 1960s through the 1970s. With his Beatlesque mop top of brown hair, trademark floppy socks, and a deadeye shot that earned him the nickname "Pistol," Pete Maravich remains a favorite to many basketball fans.

Pistol Pete *averaged* 44.2 points a game throughout his storied three-year college career at Louisiana State University, but that could have easily been 50, even 60, points a game had there been a three-point line in the Sixties. Though we'll never know how many points Pete *could* have rung up each game, the point is that he could score from anywhere on the court—just like Steph Curry.

When I watched Steph's celebrated pregame routine on YouTube, I immediately thought of Pistol Pete. What you see in Steph's fundamentals—ballhandling, dribbling, passing, and shooting—looks like it came straight out of Maravich's *Homework Basketball* video series.

Since Steph grew up in a basketball family, I'm figuring those four videos—which were popular when Steph was growing up and are still the gold standard today—were played on the family VCR. Maybe those old VHS tapes got worn out from being played over and over. If so, the one-of-a-kind drills that Pete performed and explained on camera were the foundational "homework" that helped Steph become the best all-around basketball player in the game today.

Next time you watch Steph dribble between his legs or fire a perfect bounce pass to a streaking teammate, know that all that dazzling ballhandling and offensive creativity grows from the basketball DNA of a son of Serbian immigrants, born in the steel-making town of Aliquippa, Pennsylvania.

You see, before Pete Maravich came along, basketball was a much stodgier game. There was a "right way" and a "wrong way" to play. You dribbled with your strong hand and kept the ball in front of you. None of that between-the-legs stuff. Passes were made with two hands—ball to the chest and push. And forget about making no-look passes. Coaches frowned on "showtime" basketball; players who insisted on fancy dribbling and passing were labeled "hot dogs."

You made eye contact with your teammates and kept passes as short as possible. You launched jump shots the way they're "supposed" to be done: body goes straight up, both hands on the ball. Point guards were instructed to work the ball until a 15-foot jump shot at the edge of the key presented itself. The risk/reward for longer-distance shooting didn't pencil out—even if a bomb went in, the basket was never going to be worth more than two points. If a teammate was open on a cutting move, you hit him with a bounce pass and let him drive for the basket. There were no alley-oops in those days—in fact, for a while, there was no dunking at all because the NCAA banned the practice from 1967 to 1976. Can you imagine the game being played today without slam dunks?

Pistol Pete changed the whole calculus of the game, but he paid a price. As a precocious eighth grader who made his high school varsity team, he was the target of ridicule and ostracism from his teammates. It wasn't until his junior and senior years of high school that his brash style of play gained acceptance. As Maravich dribbled circles around defenders, pouring in jump shots and hitting running bank shots from every spot on the court, "Pistol Pete," as the local sportswriters tabbed him, became a blue-chip recruit. He was in the midst of a growth spurt that would take him to 6 feet, 5 inches—the perfect height for a playmaking shooting guard.

At LSU, he would become the greatest scorer in NCAA history, revolutionizing the game and then signing the largest pro contract in history. The Atlanta Hawks gave Maravich $1.9 million. . .for *five* years. These days, top players make $1.9 million a *month*—yes, times have changed that much.

To wrap up his story, Pete also became an outspoken Christian in the last few years of his life, which was cut short when he collapsed and died while playing a pickup basketball game with Dr. James Dobson and colleagues of mine at Focus on the Family. He was forty years old.

I believe you can draw a straight line from Pistol Pete, the original ballhandling artist and shooter, forward through time to Steph Curry. Yes, Maravich was ahead of his time, and we should be grateful for that—because without him paving the way, Steph wouldn't be painting the incredible tableaus that make the Warriors star so enjoyable to watch.

"I'd say that Pistol's spirit has been passed down through Curry," declared Cedric Maxwell, an NBA teammate of Pistol Pete's. "Pete used to put on ballhandling clinics. There's a lot of that in Curry's game."

THE BEST REGULAR SEASON EVER

During the 2015–16 season, after that amazing 24–0 start, Golden State would win seven or eight games, lose one, and then start another win streak. When the Warriors became the fastest team to reach 50 wins (against only 5 losses), I thought they were a cinch to eclipse the Chicago Bull's 72–10 record set twenty years earlier.

But it wasn't easy. With a week to go in the regular season, a poor outing against the Minnesota Timberwolves, who would win only 29 games, left the margin of error at zero. If the Warriors were going to exceed the Bulls' record, they would have to win their last four games. Call it the Quest for 73.

Golden State started with a convincing 112–101 victory at home against the San Antonio Spurs, a quality team. A 100–99 victory on the road against the Memphis Grizzlies was a nail-biter—and the Warriors stole that one. A come-from-behind win *in* San Antonio left the team just one win away from the record. Then a rematch with the Grizzlies at Oracle Arena was a 125–104 blowout coronation. Steph led all scorers with 46 points.

For the 2015–16 campaign, Steph set so many records that it's hard to keep track of them all. Pundits say he had the greatest individual season in NBA history. He led the league in scoring with 30.1 points per game, but he did it while averaging fewer than 35 minutes a game. He shattered his own three-point record, hitting 402 treys, *40 percent more* than his previous record! According to FiveThirtyEight, a statistical website started by Nate Silver, that would be like Willie Mays hitting 103 home runs in a season.

Steph also broke Kyle Korver's record of most consecutive games with a three-pointer, which was 127. Steph reached 152 games by the end of the 2015–16 regular season, and looks to extend that streak in 2016–17. For good measure, he tied the NBA record for most three-point shots made in a game (12). And if you like quick hands, Steph quietly led the NBA in steals with 169.

An esoteric stat I had never heard of was the "50-40-90," representing Steph's shooting percentages from the field (.504), beyond the arc (.454), and the free throw line (.908). He became the seventh man in NBA history to put up those excellent figures, despite the fact that he jacked up more three-point attempts than anyone else in NBA history (886).

That last figure is another example of how Steph is changing the way basketball is played. For a long time, a three-pointer was a novelty shot, with entire *teams* trying as many as Steph Curry shot in 2015–16. Back in 1997–98, NBA teams averaged 12.7 three-point attempts per game, but that nearly doubled to 24.1 during the 2015–16 season. As a frame of reference, Steph himself averaged

10.9 attempts per game in 2015–16.

Because of all the numbers, I wouldn't blame you if your eyes are glazing over. So I'll cut to the chase: Is Steph the greatest shooter ever?

"The general consensus is that he's probably the best shooter this country has ever seen," said Pat Williams of the Orlando Magic. That's not a universal feeling—you can find respected basketball people like Scottie Pippen of the Chicago Bulls who say yes, while Scottie's old coach, Phil Jackson, doesn't think Steph is all that special.

I don't think we can say that Steph is the greatest shooter *ever*—not quite yet. But my prediction is that by the time Steph hangs up his sneakers, he will be generally hailed as the greatest shooter in NBA history, which dates back to 1946.

Ron Higgins is a longtime sportswriter at the *New Orleans Times-Picayune* who saw Pete Maravich play, and his dad was the sports information director at LSU during Pete's glory years. I like what he had to say about Steph:

> *If The Pistol were alive today, he'd probably admit that Curry is a better shooter than himself, maybe the best shooter ever.*
>
> *Better than Reggie Miller, Ray Allen, Larry Bird, Dale Ellis, the Person brothers Chuck and Wesley, Curry's father Dell, Curry's Warriors' coach Steve Kerr, and former European star Oscar Schmidt, whose mantra was, "A good shot is one that can be taken anywhere at anytime."*
>
> *Few players in NBA history, if any, had a quicker release or a deeper range than Curry does.*
>
> *Just on the basis of Curry's pro career regular season stats—47.7 percent from the field (a ridiculous number for a guard), 44.2 three-point percentage and 90.1 percent free throws—his shooting accuracy is in a universe by itself.*

THE PLAYOFFS

One thing everyone could agree on during the 2015–16 regular season was that Steph was the most valuable player in the league. In fact, Steph became the first NBA player to win the MVP award unanimously, as announced during the second round of the 2016 NBA Playoffs.

At the time, the Warriors were up 2–0 in their best-of-seven series against the Portland Trailblazers. Steph, though, was watching from the bench, in the midst of a two-week layoff after suffering a knee sprain in Game 4 of Golden State's opening series against the Rockets.

In Houston, like a deer skittering on a sheet of ice, Steph's feet hit a slippery patch and his legs splayed awkwardly. He grabbed at his right knee immediately. When Steph caught his breath and assessed what his knee was telling him, the news was not good. He limped off the court.

After two weeks of treatment, Steph was cleared to return to action against the Blazers, who had won Game 3 and were looking to knock off the defending champs. Steph entered Game 4 in Portland in the middle of the first quarter and looked rusty. He was only supposed to play 25 minutes and ease himself back into top-flight competition, but the way Portland fought in that pivotal game made things too close for comfort. Game 4 went to overtime, where Steph took over. Scoring an incredible 17 points, mostly on three-point shots, he secured a hard-fought win that helped the Warriors advance to the Western Conference Finals against the Oklahoma City Thunder.

"Steph was in torch mode," said Klay Thompson in the on-court postgame interview. To put those 17 points in a five-minute OT in perspective, if Steph scored like that over a complete 48-minute game, he would tally 163 points, obliterating Wilt Chamberlain's all-time record of 100 in a game, set in 1962.

With Portland out of the way, Oklahoma City loomed. I feared the Thunder because of two outstanding players: Kevin Durant and Russell Westbrook, the latter who had a basketball-sized chip on his shoulder. From the opening minute of Game 1, the pair seemed to play with extra motivation. They weren't going to take any guff.

A Game 1 victory by Oklahoma City nullified Golden State's home court advantage. The Warriors restored order and won Game 2, but then a pair of blowouts in front of insanely loud crowds in Oklahoma City pushed Golden State to the brink of a dark abyss. Down 3–1 in the series, the odds were clearly against Steph and his teammates—only nine out of 200-plus teams in NBA history had ever dug themselves out of such a deep hole. That's a success rate of about 4 percent.

Lose, and a 73-win season goes down the drain.

A home victory in Game 5, however, had the fans chanting "See You Monday," in anticipation of a Memorial Day showdown in Game 7. But winning Game 6 in KD and Westbrook's lair was a big ask, especially after Durant hit a tough midrange jumper to put the Thunder ahead 96–89 with 5:09 to go. It seemed like Golden State had been behind by six or seven points the entire game.

In golf terms, it was time to grind—keep your head down, concentrate, and go to work. Lethal shots by the Splash Brothers cut the margin. A few defensive gems from Draymond Green and Andre Iguodala provided an opening. Golden State eked out a small lead, 104–101, and Steph had the ball with 18 seconds left. He saw an opening and drove down the right side, but to get the ball over the outstretched arm of Serge Ibaka, he had to fall away to his right and kiss the ball high off the glass. . .one of his more incredible and innovative shots.

He made the shot, and that was the series. Sure, Golden State had to win Game 7, and a double-digit Thunder lead in the first half wasn't welcome—but the Warriors slowly but surely reeled in the visitors. Golden State ultimately built an 11-point lead in the fourth quarter, but Oklahoma City whittled that down to just four points with 1:18 to go. Then Ibaka—given the thankless task of defending Steph—made a big mistake: he fouled Steph, who was shooting a hurried three-pointer. That sent the NBA MVP to the free throw line for *three* shots.

With his mouthpiece dangling, Steph calmly sank all three free throws, and that—coupled with burying a three-pointer from the right wing with 26 seconds to go—sealed an exhilarating finish. Golden State's 96–88 win advanced the Warriors to the NBA Finals.

Waiting on the other side was another team with something to prove: the Cleveland Cavs. This rematch of the 2015 Finals figured to be full of great plays and intense drama.

I was impressed that Golden State took the first two games at home (*They're halfway there!*), but then Steph's team took a haymaker to the chin and lost by *thirty*—a 120–90 blowout in Game 3. How would the team get off that mat for Game 4?

This is what I think the Golden State players were thinking in the locker room: *If we don't win Game 4, it's 2–2 in the series and we might not be able to stop these guys.*

Steph had been quiet for most of the series. Even in the two home victories, he and Klay weren't doing much "splashing" as the Cavs' defense paid attention to switching off ball screens and trap pick-and-rolls to deny the Brothers three-point opportunities. Steph had only 11 points in Game 1, and Klay scored just 9. Game 2 was muted as well: Steph with 18 points and Klay with 17, most as he got hot in the second half. The blogosphere lit up Steph with headlines like: WILL THE REAL MVP PLEASE STAND UP?

Needing to rebound from the humbling Game 3 defeat, the Splash Brothers rained fire in Cleveland, hitting 11 three-pointers to contribute to a team total of 17, the most ever for the NBA Finals. With a fourth-quarter surge, the Warriors broke open a tight game to win 108–97. The ABC announcing crew reminded viewers that no team in NBA history had ever come back from a 3–1 deficit in the NBA Finals. The Cleveland "title drought" was as strong as ever.

But with Draymond Green suspended for Game 5 for accumulating four flagrant fouls, winning Game 5 at home wouldn't be easy. After Cleveland rolled to a 112–97 victory, I said to myself, *Uh-oh. This series is not done yet.* Cleveland would be tough to beat at home again, and if the series went to Game 7, something told me that LeBron James would make good on his two-year-old promise to bring a major professional sports championship home to northeast Ohio.

Game 6 in Cleveland was a rocker. . .in that Steph's world was rocked. A first-quarter mauling by the Cavs pretty much put the game out of reach when LeBron and the gang staked a 31–11 lead. Still, the Warriors fought hard to get the deficit down by seven in the second half. In the fourth quarter, LeBron came out of nowhere to fly-swat Steph's lay-in out of bounds. The play prompted a wry smirk from LeBron, video of which will be replayed thousands of times in the future.

But I was riveted by what happened with the Cavs safely ahead, 99–87, and a little less than five minutes remaining. Steph was called for a ticky-tack foul, reaching for a ball that LeBron had grabbed. Trouble was that it was Steph's sixth foul.

Steph blew his top after the call. He reached for his famous mouth guard, flinging it toward the scorer's table in frustration. Unfortunately for Steph, he missed and "hit" a fan. . .*Danger, incoming mouth guard.*

The ref slapped a technical foul on Steph, who was automatically ejected from the game—a first for him! Ralph Walker walked Steph off the court to a rain of boos, accompanying him on the long walk to the visitor's locker room.

Things got even more interesting after the game, when Ayesha took to Twitter to stand by her man:

I've lost all respect sorry this is absolutely rigged for money...
Or ratings in not sure which. I won't be silent. Just saw it live sry.

You gotta love her spunk, but she quickly apologized and deleted the tweet—not before it was shared 84,000 times—saying she "tweeted in the heat of the moment because the call was uncalled for." And then she tweeted that her father had been racially profiled after the game and threatened with arrest.

This was the backstory as both teams prepared for an epic Game 7, billed as series-decider for the ages because of the LeBron vs. Steph matchup. People were also commenting on the fact that each team had scored the same number of points—610—through the first six games.

I didn't think we'd witnessed an epic *series* because none of the six games had been close. Going into Game 7, it seemed to me that all the momentum was with LeBron James, who was determined to fulfill his promise to bring a championship to Cleveland *and* to make history as part of the first team to overcome a 3–1 deficit in the NBA Finals.

The biggest thing going for the Warriors? Their home-court advantage, playing Game 7 in front of their boisterous fans, some of whom paid record prices to witness the game. Ticket reseller Stubhub.com sold the most expensive tickets in its 16-year history when some rich cat paid $99,000 for a pair of courtside seats. Other close-to-the-floor seats sold for $25,000 each, so there was probably some Silicon Valley money being thrown around.

Golden State started off pretty well in the first quarter—something the team had not been doing for a while—but they should have been up by eight or ten points if a few more shots had fallen. The fact is, throughout the first half, Golden State was living off the three-point shots of Draymond Green, who had a really hot hand from long range in the second quarter. Golden State carried a 49–42 lead into halftime, but I felt the Warriors needed to be up by twelve or fourteen. Everyone knew that LeBron and the Cavs would make a big push at the end.

The Warriors did a good job putting Cleveland in a third-quarter hole, getting the lead up to nine at one point. Just when it looked like the home team might pop the game wide open, the Cavs went on an 11-0 run. The Warriors clung to a 76–75 lead entering the final period.

The game seesawed in the fourth quarter, and then I saw something I hadn't really seen before—Steph showed that he was human, pervious to pressure like the rest of us. With the score 89–89, he was working the ball with his left hand beyond the three-point line with his back to the basket. Suddenly, he whipped a behind-the-back pass in the direction of Klay Thompson with his *left* hand. The trouble is no one was even near the pass, which sailed out of bounds.

This was an uncharacteristic mental lapse—a brain freeze. Every athlete, from the pros on down, is coached to stick to the fundamentals when the game is on the line. I mean, here it was. . .Game 7, late in the fourth quarter, tied score, and you're whipping no-look, behind-the-back passes?

"I was aggressive in the wrong ways," Steph said immediately after the game. "It will haunt me for a while."

Inexplicably, Golden State would not score in almost the last five minutes of the game. Steph missed his final five shots. And LeBron and Kyrie Irving came through when it mattered most:

- LeBron dropping from the sky to pin Andre Iguodala's lay-in to the backboard with 1:50 to go to keep the game tied.

- Irving, with 53 seconds to go and the score *still* 89–89, working one-on-one against Steph from beyond the three-point line when he suddenly leaped and buried a long jumper over Steph's outstretched fingertips. His swish gave Cleveland a 92–89 lead that turned out to be the final nail in Golden State's coffin.

What a bummer for Dubs fans. The best team ever failed to win the NBA championship. The best three-point team of all time lost on a three-pointer. And the Warriors lost as many games in the playoffs as in the regular season.

"It hurts, man," Steph told the media afterward. "I mean, that's all I'm really kind of marinating on right now. Just proud of every single guy that stepped foot on the floor for our team this year. It wasn't easy what we accomplished, and it's not easy pill to swallow what we didn't accomplish. So got to just take the good with the bad. Understand that we hopefully will have many more opportunities to fight for championships and be on this stage because it is what it's all about."

LOOKING AHEAD

I'm not worried about Steph. He'll be back. He'll learn from his mistakes with humility and grace.

"Yeah, it stung," Steph said after losing the 2016 NBA Finals. "It sucked to watch them celebrate, and we wished that would have been us. But at the end of the day, you congratulate them for accomplishing what they set out to do, and it will be a good image for us over the summer and all next season to remember so that we can come back stronger."

Looks like the Dubs will be *much* stronger. Two weeks after the painful Game 7 loss, the basketball world was shocked as well as rocked when the Warriors announced the free-agent signing of Kevin Durant, part of the Big Three triumvirate of basketball royalty in the NBA.

During the Fourth of July weekend, Durant was holed up in his Hamptons mansion on Long Island, east of New York City. One after another, six teams made their best pitch. Oklahoma City, where Durant had played for the last nine years, desperately wanted to keep the face of their franchise. The Los Angeles Clippers, thought to be one superstar away from an NBA title, held out a blank check written by owner Steve Ballmer, the billionaire Microsoft mogul. The Boston Celtics brought in Patriots quarterback Tom Brady to convince Durant to play on the storied parquet floor at TD Garden.

The Golden State Warriors were one of the six teams invited to the KD sweepstakes. When the doorbell rang for the arrival of the Warriors' contingent in the Hamptons, Durant opened up his front door—and saw Steph, Klay Thompson, Draymond Green, and Andre Iguodala standing there, sporting wide grins.

The fact that the heart of the Warriors' team would fly across the country, on a holiday weekend, to be part of the team's presentation spoke, well, volumes. Durant was blown away. "They all walked in, and it looked like they were holding hands," Durant said afterward. "I could tell they enjoyed being around each other."

Amid such bonhomie, the Warriors leadership team ditched the video presentation. Instead, Durant's agent looked to the visiting players and asked them why they wanted his guy on their team. The first player the agent locked eyes with was Steph.

Steph didn't hesitate, just like when a three-point shot is there for the taking. Turning toward Kevin, whom he'd played against since they were ten-year-olds on AAU travel teams, Steph said, "I'm here," he said. "I want you."

This was a *kumbaya* moment. At the end of the presentation and freewheeling discussion, bro hugs were shared, hands were slapped, and the meeting ended as well as anyone from the Warriors organization could have hoped for.

A day or two later, after Durant exchanged follow-up texts with Steph and accepted a long phone call from team adviser Jerry West, the former Thunder star agreed to a two-year, $54.3 million contract with the Warriors and set the NBA world on tilt.

The 73-9 season record may be in jeopardy again. The story lines on the marriage of the Steph-led Warriors to Kevin Durant will likely dominate the 2016–17 NBA season.

What will also be interesting is what team owner Joe Lacob decides to do about offering a contract extension to Steph. The 2016–17 season is the last of his four-year contract with the team. Steph is scheduled to make $12.1 million, still the fifth-highest on the team. Since newcomer Kevin Durant is receiving more than *twice* as much at $27 mil per year, I would imagine that Steph's agent, Jeff Austin, will state the obvious and say that $27 million is the floor and negotiate up from there.

My guess is that a deal will be made and Steph will stay in the San Francisco Bay Area. . .and we'll see how things work out playing alongside Kevin Durant.

I can't wait to see what happens, but I'm sure Steph and his teammates will entertain us with enthralling basketball. You see, this is what I think Steph's greatest legacy will be—bringing fans to the NBA, a lot of new ones as well as a lot of old fans like myself, coming back to pro hoops.

For a long time, the NBA was all about power dunks and porous defense. The "product," as they say, wasn't that good—or at least like it used to be in the days of Magic Johnson and Larry Bird or Wilt Chamberlain and Bill Russell. But Steph has changed all that with his long-distance shooting that stretches the floor and allows more passing. That is what he will be remembered for.

So keep on shooting from afar, Steph.

Just watch those behind-the-back passes.

The joy of victory between Steph and teammate Andre Iguodala was evident after winning the 2015 NBA Finals over the Cleveland Cavaliers. The Warriors team hopes to replicate that feeling in the future with the addition of superstar Kevin Durant to their starting lineup.

(AP PHOTO/PAUL SANCYA)

SOURCE MATERIAL

INTRODUCTION

"'Clearly because of his injury, there was more risk there'. . ." from "Warriors' Stephen Curry Finally Has His Step Back," by Marc J. Spears, *Yahoo Sports*, December 12, 2012, and available at http://sports.yahoo.com/news/warriors--stephen-curry-finally-has-his-step-back-173207002.html

"Stephen breathed a sigh of relief. . ." from "Warriors' Stephen Curry Finally Has His Step Back," by Marc J. Spears, *Yahoo Sports*, December 12, 2012, and available at http://sports.yahoo.com/news/warriors--stephen-curry-finally-has-his-step-back-173207002.html

"'I make a lot of different cuts'. . ." from "Superstars Curry, Westbrook Rise Above Injury Concerns," by Shaun Powell, NBA.com website, December 18, 2014, and available at http://www.nba.com/2014/news/features/shaun_powell/12/18/stephen-curry-russell-westbrook-bouncing-back-well-from-early-injury-concerns/index.html?ls=iref:nbahpt3a

CHAPTER 1: HIS FATHER'S APPRENTICE

"Sonya's kin, the Snell family, is 'perhaps the most athletically decorated bloodline'. . ." from "Curry Rooted in Storied New River Valley Family Tree," by Travis Williams, *Roanoke Times*, June 14, 2015, and available at http://www.roanoke.com/news/local/radford/curry-rooted-in-storied-new-river-valley-family-tree/article_a9337524-19d8-5129-9b05-5099e91b13d6.html

"'She's a strong woman,' Steph said. . ." from "Mom Set Stephen Curry on Winning Path," by Ann Killion, *SFGate*, May 11, 2013, and available

at http://www.sfgate.com/warriors/article/Mom-set-Stephen-Curry-on-winning-path-4508899.php

"The role of disciplinarian generally fell on Sonya's shoulders. . ." from "Kid Curry," by Joshua Cooley, *Clubhouse* magazine, March 2012, and available at http://www.clubhousemagazine.com/extras/curry

"'If we didn't handle that business, there were no privileges'. . ." from "Golden State Warriors Media Conference," *ASAP Sports*, May 4, 2015, and available at http://asapsports.com/show_conference.php?id=108794

"'It says, *Look at me, I made it, I'm going to let you look at me*'. . ." from "NBA Finals: Stephen Curry's Parents Say Warriors Star Grounded by Family, Faith," by Julia Prodis Sulek, *The Mercury News*, June 6, 2015, and available at http://www.mercurynews.com/warriors/ci_28265760/nba-finals-stephen-currys-parents-say-warriors-star

"Here's what happened next, according to Warriors general manager Bob Myers. . ." from "Golden State Warriors Media Conference," *ASAP Sports*, May 4, 2015, and available at http://asapsports.com/show_conference.php?id=108794

"'We believe God opened the door for Stephen for a reason—to be a light and example of God,' she said. . ." from "NBA Finals: Stephen Curry's Parents Say Warriors Star Grounded by Family, Faith," by Julia Prodis Sulek, *The Mercury News*, June 6, 2015, and available at http://www.mercurynews.com/warriors/ci_28265760/nba-finals-stephen-currys-parents-say-warriors-star

"'We decided early on that we wouldn't focus on that with our kids'. . ." from "Mom Set Stephen Curry on Winning Path," by Ann Killion, *SFGate*, May 11, 2013, and available at http://www.sfgate.com/warriors/article/Mom-set-Stephen-Curry-on-winning-path-4508899.php

"This is how Michael Kruse of *Charlotte Magazine* described it. . ." from "Staying Stephen," by Michael Kruse, *Charlotte Magazine*, November 1, 2008, and available at http://www.charlottemagazine.com/Charlotte-Magazine/November-2008/Staying-Stephen/index.php?cparticle=2&siarticle=1

"His grandfather's unstable rim and shaky backboard became a visionary place for Steph. . ." from "Stephen Curry: The Full Circle," by David Fleming, *ESPN The Magazine*, April 23, 2015, and available at http://espn.go.com/espn/feature/story/_/id/12728744/how-golden-state-warriors-stephen-curry-became-nba-best-point-guard

"'I could always shoot because I worked on it'. . ." from "Curry Family Shooting Lineage Can Be Traced Back to Barn in Virginia," by DeAntae Prince, *Sporting News*, September 15, 2014, and available at http://www.sportingnews.com/nba/news/curry-family-dell-curry-stephen-curry-seth-curry-hornets-warriors-virginia-tech-davidson-duke/yefcjxcqohww1oiiwz4mde9nb

"'He's the kind of man I'd like to marry'. . . " from "NBA Finals: Stephen Curry's Parents Say Warriors Star Grounded by Family, Faith," by Julia Prodis Sulek, *The Mercury News*, June 6, 2015, and available at http://www.mercurynews.com/warriors/ci_28265760/nba-finals-stephen-currys-parents-say-warriors-star

CHAPTER 2: SHOOTING FROM THE HIP

"'Every coach that they had welcomed the family atmosphere'. . ." from "As Stephen Curry's Legacy Continues to Grow, Those Around Here Will Always Remember His Local Basketball Roots," by Richard Walker, *Gaston Gazette*, December 24, 2015, and available at http://www.gastongazette.com/article/20151224/NEWS/151229606

"'When Stephen was five, he could play with the eight-year-olds'. . ." from "The Steph Curry Origin Story," by Roland Lazenby, *Vice Sports*, June 8, 2015, and available at https://sports.vice.com/ca/article/the-steph-curry-origin-story

"'With Dell on the sidelines applauding'. . ." from "Charlotte Saw Stephen Curry Grow from 'Scrawny Kid' to NBA MVP," by Langston Wertz Jr. and Rick Bonnell, *Charlotte Observer*, May 4, 2015, and available at http://www.charlotteobserver.com/sports/nba/charlotte-hornets/article20022550.html

"'He never really coached me like that, to be honest'. . ." from "Stephen Curry Has Big Faith in This Private Coaching Startup," by Daniel Roberts, *Fortune*, July 30, 2015, and available at http://fortune.com/2015/07/30/coachup-private-coaching-stephen-curry/

"'I remember it like it was yesterday'. . ." from "Golden State's Stephen Curry: 'I Gave My Life to Christ,' " by Stephen Curry, cnsnews.com, June 17, 2015, and available at http://www.cnsnews.com/commentary/cnsnewscom-staff/golden-states-stephen-curry-i-gave-my-life-christ

"Lackey was out of ideas. . ." from "Northern Touch: Steph Curry's Toronto Connection," by Dave Zarum, *Sportsnet* magazine, December 5, 2013, and available at http://www.sportsnet.ca/basketball/nba/northern-touch-steph-currys-toronto-connection/

"'He taught me great lessons,' Steph said of Vince. . ." from "Q+A: Stephen Curry," by Marcel Mutoni, *Slam*, February 19, 2016, and available at http://www.slamonline.com/nba/all-star-2016/qa-stephen-curry/#p5OVFzozREtUUPoj.97

"'He was just this little, small-type kid'. . . from "The Right Steph," by Joe Posnanski, NBC Sports website, and available at http://sportsworld.nbcsports.com/stephen-curry-self-made/

"'Sometimes, kids don't pass the eye test'. . ." from "How Stephen Curry Went from Ignored

College Recruit to Possible NBA MVP," by Pat Forde, *Yahoo Sports*, April 23, 2015, and available at http://sports.yahoo.com/news/how-stephen-curry-went-from-ignored-college-recruit-to-possible-nba-mvp-011555328.html

"'And I'm watching him,' McKillop said. 'And I see it. Through it all, he never once stopped playing defense'. . ." from "The Right Steph," by Joe Posnanski, NBC Sports website, and available at http://sportsworld.nbcsports.com/stephen-curry-self-made/

"'And all of a sudden,' McKillop told Joe Posnanski of NBC Sports. . ." from "The Right Steph," by Joe Posnanski, NBC Sports website, and available at http://sportsworld.nbcsports.com/stephen-curry-self-made/

CHAPTER 3: HELLO, BASKETBALL WORLD

"'Wait until you see Stephen Curry'. . . from "How Stephen Curry Went from Ignored College Recruit to Possible NBA MVP," by Pat Forde, *Yahoo Sports*, April 23, 2015, and available at http://sports.yahoo.com/news/how-stephen-curry-went-from-ignored-college-recruit-to-possible-nba-mvp-011555328.html

"'Hey, number 30! This is a college game!'. . ." from "Ex-NBA Shooter's Son Is a Star Frosh at Davidson," by Kyle Whelliston, ESPN.com, December 20, 2006, and available at http://espn.go.com/mens-college-basketball/columns/story?id=2703294

"And then Sonya said something else in her text. . ." from "NBA Star, Charlotte Native Stephen Curry and Family Sit Down with WBTV," by Paul Cameron, WBTV.com, April 27, 2015, and available at http://www.wbtv.com/story/28913109/nba-star-charlotte-native-stephen-curry-and-family-sit-down-with-wbtv

"'Philippians 4:13 was one that I thought about when I started to play basketball all the time,' he said. . ." from "Stephen Curry Talks about His Faith with *Prodigal* Magazine," Blessed and Fresh website, and available at http://blessedandfresh.com/post/42718073056/stephen-curry-talks-about-his-faith-with-prodigal

"'I love to point people toward the Man'. . ." from "Stephen Curry: 'I Can Do All Things Through Christ,' " by Charles Chandler, Billy Graham Evangelistic Association, April 19, 2016, and available at http://billygraham.org/story/stephen-curry-i-can-do-all-things-through-christ/

"'Basically it means "have a heart for God," ' Steph said. . ." from "Steph Curry, on His Many Quirks, in His Own Words," by Tim Kawakami, *The Mercury News*, May 13, 2016, and available at http://blogs.mercurynews.com/kawakami/2016/05/13/steph-curry-quirks/

"'You could sit down and have a conversation with them [the other students] and thank them for coming to the game,' Steph said. . ." from "Stephen Curry Talks about His Faith with *Prodigal* Magazine," Blessed and Fresh website, and available at http://blessedandfresh.com/post/42718073056/stephen-curry-talks-about-his-faith-with-prodigal

"'It was like an opening night, a star performance on Broadway,' Davidson coach Bob McKillop told the press corps. . ." from "Curry's Reliable Stroke Good for 40 as Davidson Advances to the Second Round," by the Associated Press, March 22, 2008, and available at http://espn.go.com/mens-college-basketball/recap?gameId=284000011

"'Anybody else ever hold him scoreless?' Patsos asked. . ." from "Loyola Holds Curry Scoreless, but What Was the Point?" by the Associated Press, November 26, 2008, and available at http://www.nytimes.com/2008/11/27/sports/ncaabasketball/27davidson.html

"'If you look at my body compared to some point guards and [shooting] guards, I have a lot of work to do,' he said. . ." from "Curry to

Enter Draft," by the Associated Press, April 23, 2009, and available at http://espn.go.com/nba/draft2009/news/story?id=4091745

"'This has been my dream for a long time,' he said. . ." from "Curry Goes Pro on Emotional Day," by Scott Fowler, *Charlotte Observer*, April 23, 2009, and available at http://scottfowlerobs.blogspot.com/2009/04/curry-goes-pro-on-emotional-day.html

CHAPTER 4: TRYING TO TAKE A BITE OF THE BIG APPLE

"Stevan Petrovic, writing for nbadraft.net, had this predraft assessment. . ." from "Countdown to NBA Draft," by Stevan Petrovic, nbadraft.net, December 15, 2008, and available at http://www.nbadraft.net/players/stephen-curry

"'Larry, I like you a lot and respect you a lot, but don't take Steph'. . ." from "The Story of How Stephen Curry's Agent and Dad Didn't Want the Warriors to Draft Him," by Marc J. Spears, *Yahoo Sports*, May 4, 2015, and available at http://sports.yahoo.com/news/the-story-of-how-stephen-curry-s-agent-and-dad-didn-t-want-the-warriors-to-draft-him-023517645.html

"Dell didn't hide his feelings in an interview with the *New York Times*. . ." from "Stephen Curry: The Rise of the MVP," by Basketball Jonez, Golden State of Mind website, May 4, 2015, and available at http://www.goldenstateofmind.com/2015/5/4/8541939/stephen-curry-NBA-mvp-2015-golden-state-warriors-award

"Dell said, 'We had no idea that they had agreed to a trade'. . ." from "Dell Curry Recalls Suns on Near-Trade for Son Stephen Curry," by Paul Coro, *AZCentral Sports*, March 2, 2016, and available at http://www.azcentral.com/story/sports/nba/suns/2016/03/01/dell-curry-recalls-suns-near-trade-son-stephen-curry/81191584/

"Here's the conventional wisdom on Monta

Ellis, as articulated by Howard Beck. . ." from "The Evolution of Monta Ellis: Mercurial Former 'Chucker' Is Thriving in Dallas" by Howard Beck, NBA senior writer, *Bleacher Report*, December 24, 2013, and available at http://bleacherreport.com/articles/1900275-the-evolution-of-monta-ellis-mercurial-former-chucker-is-thriving-in-dallas

"'Us together? No'. . ." from "Monta Ellis on Pairing with Stephen Curry: 'We Can't . . . (We're) Not Going to Win That Way" by Tim Kawakami, *The Mercury News*, September 28, 2009, and available at http://blogs.mercurynews.com/kawakami/2009/09/28/monta-ellis-on-pairing-with-stephen-curry-we-cant-not-going-to-win-that-way/

"'She tried to play me off, saying we could hang out another time if I ever back in town'. . ." from "Home Court Advantage," by Shelley Stockton, *Charlotte Observer*, January 5, 2012, and available at http://www.charlotteobserver.com/living/carolina-bride/article9074144.html

CHAPTER 5: BREAKING OUT

"'I feel like I've been doing nothing but rehabbing for two years'. . ." from "How Stephen Curry Got the Best Worst Ankles in Sports," by Pablo S. Torre, *ESPN The Magazine*, February 10, 2016, and available at http://espn.go.com/nba/story/_/id/14750602/how-golden-state-warriors-stephen-curry-got-best-worst-ankles-sports

CHAPTER 6: FROM AIR JORDANS TO CURRY ONES

"'When I moved out [to Oakland], my mom and dad came to help me'. . ." from "My Rookie Season: Steph Curry Moves to Oakland," by Stephen Curry, GQ, November 13, 2009, and available at http://www.gq.com/story/

my-rookie-season-stephen-curry-moves-to-oakland
"For example, LeBron James is riding a lifetime deal that pays him $30 million a year. . ." from "Biggest Athlete Endorsement Deals in Sports History," totalsportek.com, January 27, 2016, and available at http://www.totalsportek.com/money/biggest-endorsement-deals-sports-history/

"Nike dominates that market. . ." from "Nike Lost Stephen Curry to Under Armour Because It Got Lazy," by Matt Bonesteel, *Washington Post*, March 23, 2016, and available at https://www.washingtonpost.com/news/early-lead/wp/2016/03/23/nike-lost-stephen-curry-to-under-armour-because-it-got-lazy/

"'I was with them [Nike] for years,' Steph told ESPN. . ." from "You Won't Believe How Nike Lost Steph to Under Armour," by Ethan Sherwood Strauss, ESPN.com, March 23, 2016, and available at http://espn.go.com/nba/story/_/id/15047018/how-nike-lost-stephen-curry-armour

"Steph and Dell leaned back in their chairs. . ." from "You Won't Believe How Nike Lost Steph to Under Armour," by Ethan Sherwood Strauss, ESPN.com, March 23, 2016, and available at http://espn.go.com/nba/story/_/id/15047018/how-nike-lost-stephen-curry-armour

"According to company executive Matt Mirchin, 'young, underdog, and next'. . ." from "How Under Armour Is Building a Winning Brand," by Palbir Nijjar, *The Motley Fool*, and available at http://www.fool.com/investing/general/2015/12/21/how-under-armour-is-building-a-winning-brand.aspx

"'It represents a Bible verse I wear on my shoe,' Curry told the media. . ." from "Stephen Curry's New Basketball Sneaker Features Bible Verse," by Christine Thomasos, *Christian Post*, February 4, 2015, and available at http://www.christianpost.com/news/stephen-currys-new-basketball-sneaker-features-bible-verse-133582/

"At a school assembly—that had to be fun for the students!—Steph told the young scholars. . ." from "Stephen Curry Gives Charlotte Christian

Special Shoes," by Marty Minchin, *Charlotte Observer*, December 3, 2015, and available at http://www.charlotteobserver.com/news/local/community/south-charlotte/article47766525.html

CHAPTER 7: ON HIS KNEES AND ON HIS GUARD

"'You know guys, you may have heard about the tragedy that happened today up in Sandy Hook'. . ." from a 2016 interview of Jeff Ryan by the author.

"'Even if we pull into a city at 2 a.m. on the road, Steph and Klay are gonna sign'. . ." from "Guarding Steph: The Only Man Who Can Lock Down Curry," by Chris Ballard, *Sports Illustrated*, March 31, 2016, and available at http://www.si.com/nba/2016/03/31/stephen-curry-golden-state-warriors-ralph-walker-security?xid=nl_siextra

"'Where's Ralph Walker at? Where's Ralph?'. . ." from "Golden State Warriors Media Conference," *ASAP Sports*, May 4, 2015, and available at http://asapsports.com/show_conference.php?id=108794

"'As Curry wraps up his allotted media time'. . ." from "Nobody Gives Under Armour Credit: A Conversation with Steph Curry," by Gerald Flores, *Sole Collector*, February 22, 2016, and available at http://solecollector.com/news/2016/02/stephen-curry-under-armour-interview

CHAPTER 8: A ROUTINE WORTHY OF BROADWAY

"'When you wake up from a nap, you know what time it is'. . ." from "Napping on Game Day Is Prevalent Among NBA Players," by Jonathan Abrams, *New York Times*, March 6, 2011, and available at http://www.nytimes.com/2011/03/07/sports/basketball/07naps.html?pagewanted=all&_r=1

"Fans seeking the experience unwittingly raised the average ticket resale price..." from "Stephen Curry: The NBA's Must-See Player—Even in Practice," by Ben Cohen, *Wall Street Journal*, December 3, 2015, and available at http://www.wsj.com/articles/stephen-curry-the-nbas-must-see-playereven-in-practice-1449159190

"Steph's reaction was succinct..." from "Stephen Curry: Kerr Move a Surprise," by the Associated Press, May 29, 2014, and available at http://espn.go.com/nba/story/_/id/11002396/stephen-curry-golden-state-warriors-disagrees-mark-jackson-firing

"'Congratulations to him,' he replied, referring to Kerr..." from "Mark Jackson on Steve Kerr," by Tim Kawakami, *The Mercury News*, May 15, 2014, and available at http://blogs.mercurynews.com/kawakami/2014/05/15/mark-jackson-on-steve-kerr-steph-currys-response-tweeting-about-stan-van-gundy-and-the-real-meaning-of-the-mafia-suit/

"'She had that look, like she wasn't going to take no for an answer'..." from "Exclusive: Stephen Curry and Wife Ayesha on Marriage, Kids, and Their Matching Tattoos," by Alan Shipnuck, *Parents* magazine, June 2016, and available at http://www.parents.com/parenting/celebrity-parents/moms-dads/stephen-curry-wife-ayesha-on-marriage-kids-matching-tattoos/

"'I was blown away by her recipes, her voice, and her strong point of view'..." from "Ayesha Curry Is Having Fun Proving People Wrong," by Darren Rovell, ESPN.com, June 7, 2016, and available at http://espn.go.com/espnw/culture/feature/article/16002785/ayesha-curry-exclusive-interview-having-fun-proving-people-wrong

CHAPTER 9: "I'LL TAKE STEPH FOR $400, ALEX"

"'I'm in awe every time I see Stephen Curry play'..." from "Stephen Curry," by Misty Copeland, *Time* magazine, April 21, 2016, and available at http://time.com/4301269/stephen-curry-2016-time-100/

"'It was a lot of fun,' Steph said..." from "Curry Cards Three Birdies, Has 'a Blast,'" by Ron Green Jr., *Charlotte Observer*, April 26, 2010, and available at http://www.wellsfargochampionship.com/thechampionship/tournamenthistory/Archive_2010/NewsArticles_2010/Quail_Hollow_Notebook_Curry_cards_three_birdies.aspx

"'He opened up a lot about how he never really valued his anonymity until it was gone'..." from "NBA Finals MVP Stephen Curry," by Craig Bestrom, *Golf Digest*, October 29, 2015, and available at http://www.golfdigest.com/story/golfers-who-give-back-interview-with-nba-finals-mvp-stephen-curry

"'It can only go downhill from there,' Steph said..." from "Stephen Curry Even Shoots a Three at Augusta National Golf Club," by Cindy Boren, *Washington Post*, February 24, 2016, and available at https://www.washingtonpost.com/news/early-lead/wp/2016/02/24/stephen-curry-even-shoots-a-three-at-augusta-national-golf-club/

"'I've heard people say I'm a Curry and that helped me get where I am,' Seth said..." from "The Incredible Journey of Seth Curry," by Lee Jenkins, *Sports Illustrated*, September 8, 2015, and available at http://www.si.com/nba/2015/09/08/seth-curry-kings-stephen-curry-warriors

"'She never says her last name,' Elon coach Mary Tendler said..." from "Standing Out on Her Own, Elon Setter Just Wants to Sydel—Not Sydel Curry," by Jodie Valade and Don Schick, *American Sports Network*, November 26, 2015, and available at http://americansportsnet.com/standing-out-on-her-own-elon-setter-just-wants-to-be-sydel-not-sydel-curry/

"'His first year, it was really very difficult because when I watch his games I focus in on him,' Dell said..." from "Dell Curry on Stephen Curry's

54-Point Game," by James Herbert, *SB Nation*, March 1, 2013, and available at http://www.sbnation.com/nba/2013/3/1/4043014/stephen-curry-dell-curry-warriors-54-knicks-2012

"Occasionally, people make dumb jokes about Steph. . ." from "Larry Wilmore Roasts the Press in White House Correspondents' Monologue," by Matt Wilstein, *The Daily Beast*, April 30, 2016, and available at http://www.thedailybeast.com/articles/2016/04/30/larry-wilmore-roasts-the-press-in-white-house-correspondents-monologue.html

"'I don't really worry about the shots that I missed,' he said during the 2016 NBA Finals. . ." from "Stephen Curry: 'I Don't Really Worry About the Shots I Missed,' " by the Associated Press, June 16, 2016, and available at http://nba.nbcsports.com/2016/06/16/stephen-curry-i-dont-really-worry-about-the-shots-that-i-missed/

"He and fellow Splash Brother Klay Thompson 'are allowed to take any shots they want'. . ." from "Steve Kerr: Stephen Curry and Klay Thompson Can Take 'Any Shots They Want,' " by AJ Neuharth-Keusch, *USA Today*, June 5, 2016, and available at http://www.usatoday.com/story/sports/nba/2016/06/05/steve-kerr-stephen-curry-klay-thompson-nba-finals/85459540/

"'First and foremost, I have to thank my Lord and Savior Jesus Christ'. . ." from "Golden State Warriors Media Conference," *ASAP Sports*, May 4, 2015, and available at http://asapsports.com/show_conference.php?id=108794

"'I like it,' Steph said. 'I'm a competitor, so I like those kind of challenges'. . ." from "Killion: Curry Looks to Avoid Paying for His Mistakes," by Ann Killion, *San Francisco Chronicle*, January 19, 2015, and available at http://www.sfchronicle.com/warriors/article/Killion-Curry-looks-to-avoid-paying-for-his-6026207.php?t=68c8144473da9fb8e6&cmpid=twitter-premium#/0

"Asked if he can repeat the phrase in Hebrew, Steph said, 'I can't. I'm working on it'. . . from "What Is the Meaning Behind Stephen Curry's

Hebrew Tattoo?" *Jerusalem Post*, June 9, 2015, and available at http://www.jpost.com/Israel-News/Sports/What-is-the-meaning-behind-Stephen-Currys-Hebrew-tattoo-405551

"'This signifies that the past is behind us and the future is in front of us'. . . from "Exclusive: Stephen Curry and Wife Ayesha on Marriage, Kids, and Their Matching Tattoos," by Alan Shipnuck, *Parents* magazine, June 2016, and available at http://www.parents.com/parenting/celebrity-parents/moms-dads/stephen-curry-wife-ayesha-on-marriage-kids-matching-tattoos/

"Ayesha was asked by *Hello Beautiful* magazine. . ." from "4 Secrets of a Successful Marriage from Ayesha Curry," by ZD Amour, CocoaFab.com, June 15, 2015, and available at http://cocoafab.com/4-secrets-to-successful-marriage-from-ayesha-curry/

CHAPTER 10: A SEASON TO REMEMBER, A GAME 7 TO FORGET

"Hall of Famer Oscar Robertson went on ESPN's *Mike & Mike Show* to say that today's coaches didn't know anything about defense. . ." from "Stephen Curry: Criticism Starting to Get a Little Annoying," by ESPN.com news services, February 27, 2016, and available at http://espn.go.com/nba/story/_/id/14857175/golden-state-warriors-stephen-curry-finds-bashing-retired-stars-annoying

"'It's starting to get a little annoying just because it's kind of unwarranted from across the board'. . ." from "Stephen Curry: Criticism Starting to Get a Little Annoying," by ESPN.com news services, February 27, 2016, and available at http://espn.go.com/nba/story/_/id/14857175/golden-state-warriors-stephen-curry-finds-bashing-retired-stars-annoying

"Dell had the right take when asked about Oscar Robertson's comments. . ." from "Like Most

Everyone, Dell Curry Enjoying Steph's Run," by Shaun Powell, NBA.com, February 29, 2016, and available at http://www.nba.com/2016/news/features/shaun_powell/02/29/dell-curry-talks-about-stephen-currys-season-oscar-robertson-comments/

"'I'd say that Pistol's spirit has been passed down through Curry'. . ." from "Is Stephen Curry a Latter-Day Pete Maravich?" by Bob Ryan, *Boston Globe*, March 12, 2016, and available at https://www.bostonglobe.com/sports/2016/03/12/bob-ryan-stephen-curry-latter-day-pete-maravich/6c9bPpNIh1tE1bBPDH0gcl/story.html

"'If The Pistol were alive today, he'd probably admit that Curry is a better shooter than himself'. . ." from "Steph Curry Is the New 'Next' Pistol Pete but No One Tops the Original," by Ron Higgins, *The Times-Picayune*, January 22, 2016, and available at http://www.nola.com/lsu/index.ssf/2016/01/steph_curry_is_the_new_next_pi.html

"'I was aggressive in the wrong ways,' Steph said immediately after the game. . ." from "48 Minutes for 52 Years as LeBron Completes His Mission," by Josh Weir, *Times Reporter*, June 20, 2016, and available at http://www.timesreporter.com/sports/20160620/josh-weir-48-minutes-for-52-years-as-lebron-completes-his-mission

"'It hurts, man,' Steph told the media afterward…" from "Stephen Curry 'Haunted' by Game 7 Performance," by Dejan Kalinic, *The Sporting News*, June 20, 2016, and available at http://www.sportingnews.com/nba/news/stephen-curry-warriors-nba-finals-game-7/bwo0jcevt42r1r6c8krrkjj1p

"'Yeah, it stung,' Steph said after losing the 2016 NBA Finals. . ." from "Warriors' Curry, Iguodala Don't Intend to Forget," by Tim Kawakami, *The Mercury News*, June 20, 2016, and available at http://www.mercurynews.com/tim-kawakami/ci_30035520/kawakami-warriors-curry-iguodala-dont-intend-forget

"'They all walked in, and it looked like they were holding hands'. . ." from "Heist in the Hamptons: How the Warriors Landed Durant," by Kevin Jones, KNBR.com, July 7, 2016, and available at http://www.knbr.com/2016/07/07/heist-in-the-hamptons-how-the-warriors-won-kevin-durant/

ABOUT THE AUTHOR

MIKE YORKEY is the author or coauthor of more than one hundred books with more than two million copies in print. His latest book is *After the Cheering Stops* with Cyndy Feasel, telling the tragic story of her family's journey into chaos and darkness resulting from the damage her husband, Grant Feasel of the Seattle Seahawks, suffered due to football-related concussions and head trauma.

Mike has also collaborated with the Chicago Cubs' Ben Zobrist and his wife, Julianna, a Christian music artist, in *Double Play*; Washington Redskins quarterback Colt McCoy and his father, Brad, in *Growing Up Colt*; San Francisco Giants pitcher Dave Dravecky in *Called Up*; San Diego Chargers placekicker Rolf Benirschke in *Alive & Kicking*; tennis star Michael Chang in *Holding Serve*; and paralyzed Rutgers' defensive tackle Eric LeGrand in *Believe: My Faith and the Tackle That Changed My Life*. Mike is also the coauthor of the internationally bestselling Every Man's Battle series with Steve Arterburn and Fred Stoeker.

He and his wife, Nicole, are the parents of two adult children and make their home in Encinitas, California.

Mike's website is www.mikeyorkey.com.

Love Sports and the Outdoors?
Check Out. . .

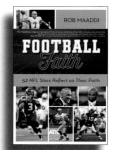

Football Faith by Rob Maaddi

Football Faith will inspire and encourage readers in their faith journey, as 52 NFL players share their stories and how they are chasing the success that only comes from being God's man and following His plan. Featuring personal stories from Russell Wilson, Aaron Rodgers, Colin Kaepernick, Deion Sanders, and dozens more—plus with a foreword from Coach Joe Gibbs.

Paperback / 978-1-63409-222-7 / $16.99

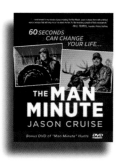

The Man Minute by Jason Cruise

Every "Man Minute" devotion is designed to be read in sixty seconds, yet a man will carry the insights he gleans into a lifelong journey of spiritual manhood. *The Man Minute* is packaged alongside a DVD featuring hunts—each couched in spiritual truths—with some of the most recognized hunters on the planet.

Hardback / 978-1-63058-718-5 / $16.99